Sir John Fortescue's
The Hardest Pounding

WELLINGTON ORDERS THE ADVANCE AT WATERLOO

Sir John Fortescue's
The Hardest Pounding

A History of the British Army During the
Campaign of 1815, Quatre Bras, and Waterloo

J. W. Fortescue

LEONAUR

Sir John Fortescue's The Hardest Pounding
A History of the British Army During the Campaign of 1815, Quatre Bras, and
Waterloo
by J. W. Fortescue

FIRST EDITION

First published under the title
A History of the British Army Vol 10 (Extract)

Leonaur is an imprint of Oakpast Ltd

Copyright in this form © 2014 Oakpast Ltd

ISBN: 978-1-78282-355-1 (hardcover)
ISBN: 978-1-78282-356-8 (softcover)

http://www.leonaur.com

Publisher's Notes

Contents

Hard pounding this, gentlemen:
but we shall see who can pound the longest.
—The Duke of Wellington

CHAPTER 1

The Gathering Storm

During the early weeks of 1815, within the British Government, Liverpool, (at Castlereagh's request), was contemplating the expulsion of Murat from Naples. The close proximity of Elba, with its infamous exile, to that state kept King Louis the Eighteenth and equally Wellington in constant apprehension.[1] The king, indeed, made the state of Italy his excuse for not paying to Napoleon a farthing of the £80,000 which the Allies had pledged him to allow to the fallen emperor; and in less than a week after the date of Liverpool's letter, on the night of Sunday the 26th of February, Napoleon embarked by stealth at Porto Ferrajo, with the four hundred men which he retained as his guard, and landed at the Golfe de Jouan on the 1st of March. Moving first upon Antibes he found his overtures repelled by the garrison; but at Grenoble he was received by the troops with wild enthusiasm, and marched thence with fourteen thousand men upon Paris.

Marshal Ney, who had set forth to capture his old master, found himself deserted by his best troops and embraced his side; and on the 20th of March Napoleon entered Paris amid wild shouts of joy from discharged soldiers and from officers who were starving on their half-pay.

King Louis, abandoned by the army, whose work this revolution really was, fled first to Lille and, as his prospects grew worse, was for passing over to England, but was persuaded to establish his shadow of a court at Ghent.

The Duke of Angoulême, who had collected some kind of a force about Nimes, with the object of marching on Lyons and saving at any rate the southern provinces for the monarchy, gained a trifling success on the 2nd of April, but was surrounded and compelled to capitulate

---

1. *Wellington Supp. Desp.* 9

six days later. On the 16th of April he embarked at Cette for Spain, and all royalist resistance to Napoleon in this quarter came to an end.

The Bourbons have been much blamed for their folly during the first period of their restoration, from May 1814 till March 1815, and undoubtedly they were guilty of grave mistakes. But their difficulties, from the exhausted state of the country, were stupendous; and an archangel from Heaven could not have restored even the beginning of content to France, after all her misfortunes, within a period of ten months. Yet the only true supporters of Napoleon's short second empire were the men who had been discharged in rags and the officers who had been retired on a pittance, in order to cover the reconstituted Household troops of France with gorgeous uniforms.

The news no sooner reached Vienna than the assembled plenipotentiaries drew up a public declaration that Napoleon Bonaparte had placed himself outside the pale of public law, and must be delivered to public justice as a common enemy and disturber of the peace. To this declaration Wellington, as was natural, set his hand, and was rewarded by being denounced by Whitbread in the House of Commons as one who abetted an openly expressed intention to assassinate Bonaparte; an infamous accusation which might have been excused by Whitbread's ignorance of the French language, but for which, in his portentous vanity, he had not the grace to apologise. In every capital of Europe the alarm was great; but it was speedily resolved that the plague should be abated at any cost.

On the 25th of March it was agreed between Great Britain, Russia, Prussia and Austria that, pursuant to the Treaty of Chaumont, each of these Powers should place one hundred and fifty thousand men in the field, and not lay down their arms until Bonaparte should have been rendered helpless for war. In the case of Great Britain it was arranged that she should be at liberty to substitute money for men at a fixed rate. Having signed this instrument and a further convention to grant a subsidy of five millions sterling to the contracting parties, Wellington left Vienna on the 29th of March and, travelling at great speed, reached Brussels on the night of the 4th of April. The Prince of Orange had taken alarm from the first, he had written on the 17th of March:

> Bonaparte will, I am persuaded, enter Paris very shortly. He will then move down without delay upon this frontier.

Accordingly, he had ordered the fortresses of Western Flanders and Mons to be repaired at once, so as to secure them against a stroke of surprise, and had despatched a messenger to ask for help from General Kleist, then commanding an army of rather over forty thousand Prussians and Saxons, which were stationed about Aix-la-Chapelle. The arrival of Wellington in the Netherlands was an intense relief to ministers, for the Prince of Orange, with rather absurd conceit, declared that he would not willingly have yielded up his charge to any other man. He was, in fact, burning to invade France and to fight Napoleon single-handed; and, even after receiving from Bathurst strict orders to do nothing so foolish, he had maintained his dispositions for an advance. Young and ambitious of military glory, he was still unaware, though he was shortly to prove, that he was unfit even to command a battalion. [2]

The information that greeted the Duke of Wellington upon his arrival at Brussels was not of the most cheering. Ten days before quitting Vienna he had urged the reinforcement of the army in the Netherlands to the utmost; and the answer that awaited him set forth the following facts. The entire strength of British troops which ministers could immediately place at his disposal did not exceed six regiments of cavalry and twenty-five battalions of infantry. Of these twenty-five no fewer than fifteen were the "weak corps and inefficient battalions" which had been hastily scraped together for the sudden emergency which called Graham to Holland, and which contained on an average fewer than five hundred men apiece. The three battalions of Guards were superior to the rest in strength, but even they contained four hundred men too young and weak for service in the field.

Of the ten new battalions promised to him, the third battalion of the Fourteenth had not been in existence two years, and at the outset had been rejected for active work, the Inspector-general remarking that he had never seen such a lot of boys, both officers and men. The second battalion of the Fifty-Ninth were likewise unfit for any but garrison duties, being young, half-trained and weak in numbers. Of the remainder the first battalions of the Fifty-Second, Seventy-First, and Ninety-First were embarked and sailing for America, but had been recalled and directed to Ostend; while those of the Twenty-third, Fifty-First and Ninety-Fifth were in garrison on the south coast of England.

One and all of these six had served for long in the Peninsula, though the last three had lost many of their veteran soldiers owing to

---

2. *Wellington Supp. Desp.* 9, *Le Bas*, 1.

the expiration of their term of service; and it must be added that the first battalion of the Fifty-Second, by absorbing the remnants of its second battalion, did not add to the number of units, though it added much to the strength and quality, of the troops at the front. The utmost that Ministers could hope to send, beyond this handful of men, was a brigade of heavy cavalry and four battalions of infantry from Ireland, with which the authorities at Dublin Castle were extremely reluctant to part, and a battalion of Guards, together with a few squadrons of Household Cavalry as soon as certain riots, which had arisen in London over the subject of the Corn Laws, should have subsided. It was necessary to provide for the safety of Malta, Messina and Corfu, which would strain the British resources in the Mediterranean to the utmost; and in the West Indies battalions would be required to look after Martinique and Guadeloupe. In fact, until the return of troops from America and Canada nothing more could be done towards the making of a British force in the Netherlands. [3]

Highly indignant that the British Army should be so poorly represented at so critical a time, Wellington complained bitterly that the government might liberate the soldiers in Ireland at once by calling out the Militia. But ministers were unfortunately hampered by technical difficulties, all of which turned upon the question, bluntly propounded by Whitbread in the Commons, "Are we at peace or at war?" At war with France England certainly was not and had no wish to be; but, on the other hand, she had pledged herself in concert with the Powers of Europe to suppress Napoleon Bonaparte, who had just arrogated to himself supreme authority in France and was supported by the whole of her military forces.

Now the Crown had no right to call out the Militia except in time of actual war or insurrection. As it happened, there were still seventeen thousand British Militia, complete battalions of respectable strength, embodied under the emergency of the last war which had been terminated by the first Peace of Paris; and there would have been more but for the factious clamour of the Opposition for their immediate disbandment. But of the disembodied residue so many men, both principals and substitutes, had taken their discharge on the completion of their term of service, that not above twenty thousand were left, and those were dispersed among a number of weak battalions. If those twenty thousand were summoned by reason of a new war, then all the men of the seventeen thousand, whose period of service was bounded

---

3. *Wellington Supp. Desp.* 9.

by the close of the last war, might reasonably claim their discharge.

All that would be gained therefore by the calling out of the Militia would be the substitution of fifty or sixty weak battalions, counting in all twenty thousand men, for five and twenty or thirty respectable bodies numbering only three thousand less. Ministers judged the seventeen thousand to be more valuable than the twenty thousand, and beyond doubt they were right.

Moreover, the expediency of a ballot was, in the circumstances, very doubtful. The country was full of discharged soldiers whom it was most desirable to regain for the regular army; but there was every probability that, in the event of a ballot, they would engage themselves as substitutes in the Militia, with the hope of receiving later a large bounty to transfer themselves later to the Line. The whole situation was strangely complicated, so much so that the Cabinet took seven full weeks, dating from Napoleon's entry into Paris, to come to a decision concerning it.

At last, on the 9th of May, they brought forward a Bill to permit the Local Militia to volunteer for duties in garrison, so as to release the old Militia for more important functions. A fortnight later a second Bill was introduced to draw out and embody the Old Militia itself, the preamble stating that "there was an immediate prospect of war with France"; and it was arranged that the vacancies should be filled by beat of drum, and that a moderate bounty should be offered to old soldiers who would rejoin the regiments of the Line. These two Bills quickly became law on the 14th of June, the day before Napoleon crossed the Sambre, and four days before the Battle of Waterloo. [4]

It is difficult to understand why ministers should have waited so long before setting all doubts as to the Militia Laws at rest by means of the simple preamble quoted above; and the whole of this episode brings into glaring relief the evils of our party system and the defects of our organisation, even after nearly a quarter of a century of war, for National Defence. The eulogists of Napoleon in Parliament had no real wish to see him again become a menace to Europe, still less to give him a chance of invading England; nor did they even desire their country to lose weight in the councils of Europe at the Congress of Vienna.

Yet they deliberately laid themselves out to fulfil the whole of these purposes, simply because by so doing they might embarrass the

4. Hansard, xxxi., Statutes 55, Geo. III. caps. 76, 77. *Wellington Supp. Desp.* 10., *Desp.*, to Bathurst, 6th Apr. 1815.

government. French authors continue to quote their speeches as evidence that there was a Napoleonic party in the British Parliament. There was nothing of the kind; but there was a certain number of gentlemen who, finding his name a useful counter in the game of party, did not hesitate to degrade it by turning it to that contemptible use. They deceived themselves—at least it is charitable to believe so—they deceived him, and they caused considerable anxiety to our general in the field; thus accomplishing what is probably the greatest degree of mischief that is possible to small talkers in their relation to great men.

As to the vacillation of the government in regard to the Militia, it must be remarked that the issue raised by Whitbread—whether England were at war or peace—was a real one which troubled even Wellington at the front long after the words were spoken in Parliament. He wrote to the Prince of Orange on the 11th of May:

"In the situation in which we are placed at present neither at war or at peace, unable on that account to patrol up to the enemy and ascertain his position by view or to act offensively upon any part of his line, it is difficult if not impossible to combine our operations because there are no data upon which to found a combination."

Yet the British Navy had begun to take French prizes in the Channel and on the Atlantic seaboard before the end of March. The Prince of Orange had arrested French prisoners who were on their way to France from Russia; and the Continental Powers had cut off all regular communications between France and the world without. All of these were hostile acts, and it is therefore difficult to understand why ministers should have boggled at the wording of the Militia Statutes. But be it observed that, if our system of National Defence had been based upon the compulsory personal service of every man of military age, the difficulty arising from the wholesale discharge of substitutes would not have arisen. It would have been sufficient to call out the Militia, and the ranks would automatically have been full of trained men. No system of National Defence is sound which recognises, as the British system had always recognised, the principle of substitution.

To return to Wellington's army, cavalry, from the nature of the American War, was more easily provided than infantry; and the Horse Guards had made no difficulty about the immediate despatch of six regiments of Light Horse which had served in the Peninsula. But the whole of them were weak and could send abroad only three squadrons apiece, of fewer than one hundred and fifty of all ranks to the squadron. The artillery was in a still more woeful plight. There was plenty of guns and ammunition; but, since seven thousand of the Royal Regiment had been discharged since the Peace of Paris, the master-general could provide neither men nor horses. Considering the difficulty of training gunners and drivers, this immediate and sweeping reduction of the artillery, before the Congress of Vienna had concluded its labours, was reckless in the extreme; but there the fact was.

Wellington asked for one hundred and fifty cannon, and the master-general was unprepared to supply immediately more than forty-two. Nor could he hope to furnish drivers, except by enlisting post-boys for short periods, so as to make use of those who were out of place, and by offering four guineas bounty to such Hanoverians as might condescend to accept it. [5]

Over and above the British troops, and almost to be considered as a part of them, was the King's German Legion, some corps of which had been halted in the Netherlands while on their way to Hanover for disbandment. They comprised five strong regiments of cavalry, eight weak battalions of foot, and three and a half batteries of artillery with thirty guns, of which four corps of the horse, five of the foot, and three of the artillery had served under Wellington in the Peninsula. Supplementary to the Legion were the Hanoverian Militia, consisting of one battery, two regiments of cavalry, and twenty-five battalions of infantry. These were all of them young half-trained troops, and greatly deficient in officers. As the regiments of the Legion were in want of men, Wellington proposed that they might be filled up, as in England, by volunteers from the Militia; but, this suggestion being rejected by the Hanoverian Government, he had no alternative but to reduce the battalions of the Legion from ten companies to six, and to transfer the supernumerary officers and non-commissioned officers from the Legion to the Militia.

This was a false policy, for it is easier to make good infantry by mixing young soldiers with twice their number of veterans, than by keeping the young soldiers together and adding only an infusion of old officers and sergeants; but the Hanoverians decreed that this mistake should be deliberately made, and made it was. [6]

As regards the staff, Wellington complained bitterly that he was flooded with officers who were all of them useless, he wrote:

---

5. *Wellington Supp. Desp.* 10. 6. *Wellington Desp.*, to the Prince Regent, 17th April 1815. Beamish, ii. 323 n.

I might have expected that the generals and staff formed by me in the last war would have been allowed to come to me again, but instead of that I am overloaded with people I have never seen before; and it appears to be purposely intended to keep those out of my way whom I wished to have.

As the duke repeated statements to this effect at intervals to the end of his life, it will be well to examine the matter more closely. It must be premised that the Anglo-Hanoverian force which he took over from the Prince of Orange was an organised army with its staff complete; and it will be admitted that, while it is easy to give a general a free hand in nominating his staff when every place is vacant, it is difficult, without hardship, to do so when many places are already filled up by officers who have held their posts for many months. Nevertheless the Duke of York, through Sir Henry Torrens, desired Wellington, immediately after his arrival in the Low Countries, to favour him with his wishes respecting all appointments; and Torrens himself not only wrote at once to recall Sir George Murray, who had sailed to Canada to take the place of Prevost, but privately begged the field-marshal not to hesitate, on the score of friendship, to displace a relative of his own, an old Peninsular officer, from the quartermaster-general's department. To make things still easier, Torrens repaired to the Netherlands himself to facilitate the arrangement of these and kindred matters.

The quartermaster-general to the Prince of Orange was Sir Hudson Lowe, an officer of great ability, deep professional knowledge, and very wide experience, having been present at thirteen general actions in which Napoleon in person was commanding the French. Torrens speedily discovered that Lowe "would not do for the duke"; and it was arranged that Sir Hudson should take his departure immediately upon Murray's return, and that Colonel de Lancey should be summoned to resume his old place as deputy quartermaster-general.

De Lancey demurred to the "indignity" of returning to a situation which he had so long held in the Peninsula, but presently set out for Brussels; and the removal of Lowe to a command in the Mediterranean at the end of May left De Lancey in the post, which he had desired, of Chief Staff Officer. The adjutant-general was Sir Edward Barnes, one of Wellington's brigadiers in 1813 and 1814 and an excellent man for the place. The head of the artillery was Colonel George Wood; the head of the engineers Sir James Carmichael Smyth, who had worked out the plans for the very able attack on Bergen-op-Zoom; and the commissary-general was Mr. Dunmore, who had been specially sent for from the Peninsular Army by Graham.

The divisional commanders were George Cooke, who had for some time been in charge of Cadiz and had served throughout Graham's campaign in Holland, Vandeleur, Charles Alten, and Hinüber, all of whom Wellington had known well in the Peninsula, and Victor Alten, of whom Wellington had rid himself. The brigadiers were Peregrine Maitland, who had already served with the duke in the Pyrenees; Lyon, who had commanded a battalion in Portugal until 1812 and since then a division of Hanoverians at Göhrde; Kenneth Mackenzie, a pupil of Charles Stuart and of John Moore, who had distinguished himself in various campaigns; Frederick Adam, whose fortunes, unluckily for him, had been linked to John Murray and William Bentinck; Colin Halkett, Ompteda, Arentschild, Bussche, Dörnberg, and Du Plat, all of the German Legion, of whom the first four were veterans of the Peninsula and the last two alone bore unfamiliar names.

In the case of Adam, the Duke of York represented that he was an intelligent and distinguished officer to whom a brigade had been long promised, and that, as he chanced to be in the Netherlands, he had been placed upon the staff of the army there. Yet another brigadier, Johnstone, was in command of the brigade which was on the point of starting for America when it was recalled and sent to Flanders; and it was reasonably thought unjust that he should be removed solely on account of the change of destination. So far, therefore, it does not appear that Wellington had any just grievance against the original composition of the staff of the army in the Netherlands; and it may be added that the first new names added to the list by the Duke of York were those of Hill, Colville, Clinton, and Vivian.

Passing next to the junior members of the Prince of Orange's staff, two out of five in the adjutant-general's department had served on the staff of the Peninsular Army with distinction from beginning to end; a third, after brilliant work as a regimental officer, had joined the staff in 1813; a fourth had commanded a battalion under Graham, and the fifth had been a staff-officer in the West Indies. In the quartermaster-general's department, one of the four deputies had served in that same department from the first to the last of the Peninsular War, two more had passed through the war partly as regimental and partly as staff-officers, and the fourth, having been attached to Lord Cathcart while that nobleman was commissioner with the Russian armies in 1813 and 1814, could claim at least a considerable experience of work in the field.

As the whole of these gentlemen retained their places, there seems to have been no great objection to them. When Wellington took over the army, eighteen new officers were added to the adjutant-general's department and twenty-four to the quartermaster-general's. Among the former are to be found the familiar names of Elley and Waters; and, so far as I can ascertain, nearly all of the remainder had seen service in the Peninsula, more than one of them on the staff. There is only one whose appointment suggests itself to me decidedly as a job. Among the latter are to be found Felton, Hervey, Jeremiah Dickson, Lord Greenock, Gomm and four more who had done the like work in the Peninsula and were men of tried capacity; and of the residue some certainly, and many probably, had learned at least their regimental duty in Spain and Portugal.

For the rest, the Duke of York was ready and indeed eager to send out Edward Paget, Dalhousie, Picton and Cole. Kempt, Pack, Byng, and William Ponsonby were on their way to the Low Countries. Alexander Dickson was sent out specially to do any work with the artillery that Wellington might choose to assign to him. Colquhoun Grant was spared to take charge of the department of intelligence; and McGrigor, though about to take up the duty of Director-general of Hospitals, offered to come over to headquarters and organise the medical service. In fact, of Wellington's most trusted subordinates only Murray and Burgoyne were absent, both of them in America.

Altogether, although there was undoubtedly some friction in the matter of appointments to the staff, and there may have been more young gentlemen than work could be found for, it seems to me that, except in the matter of reducing its numbers, Wellington had his own way and had no right to complain that his staff was without experience. The secret of all his ill temper seems to have been that many of his former staff-captains and majors had, by exchange into the Guards, obtained the rank of lieutenant-colonel, and were on that account at first rejected by the Duke of York, though subsequently permitted to take up their appointments. Wellington's sweeping statements therefore, on this as on some other topics, should not be accepted without much reservation. [7]

It remains to consider the Allied armies with which Wellington was

---

7. *Wellington Supp. Desp.* 10; Despatches to Torrens; to Maj.-Gen. Darling; to Lord Stewart; to Dr. Renny. *Life of Sir William Gomm.*

expected to act, both within his own command and without it. Of the Dutch troops the reports sent to him were contradictory. In general their spirit was said to be good; but many of the officers of all grades, as well as some of the men, had been in the service of France, and were suspected to be, not unnaturally, in sympathy with her. The bond of military comradeship is strong; and the French faction in Holland, notwithstanding its defeat by the bold diplomacy of Sir James Harris in 1787, had by no means been wholly extinguished.

At the head of the Ministry of War was General Janssens, who, having fought unsuccessfully against the British both at the Cape and in Java, would hardly have been human if he had felt kindly towards them; and the officers of almost every department under him were known to be at heart partisans of the revolution and of France. The exception among them was the quartermaster-general, Major-General Constant de Rebecque, a loyal, able, and energetic officer, who had accompanied the Prince of Orange throughout the campaigns in the Peninsula. The army itself was in course of reorganisation; the Dutch fortresses were in bad order; and there was a scarcity of muskets.

The Belgian troops were represented, unequivocally and not inaccurately, to be bad and untrustworthy. The creation of the army for the service of the King of the Netherlands had only begun in February 1814, and had been greatly hampered by want of funds, clothing and arms, with the inevitable consequence of much desertion. The officers were said to be friendly to the French, but the general attitude of the privates, and indeed of the whole population, was that of sulky indifference. In 1814, when the Belgians had received a promise of independence, they had rejoiced over their deliverance from the yoke of Napoleon.

But when they found their country annexed to Holland, by no will of their own but for the convenience of the mightier powers, they were filled with disgust towards European politics, and regarded with impartial hatred all the contending nations which were preparing once again to turn their fair and unhappy land into an arena for the settlement of their differences. There was no lack of brave men of all ranks among them; they had proved their courage when fighting under the standards of Napoleon; but they had no enthusiasm for the new cause for which they found themselves impressed, and they saw in it nothing worth the spending of their blood. An impartial observer is bound to admit that they were amply justified. Since the Belgians were of this stamp and the Dutch troops were mostly Militia, it was very doubtful whether they would be of great military value, whatever their appearance. Wellington after inspecting them pronounced on them the following judgment.

The Nassauers (it will be remembered that a battalion of them had deserted to the British in France) were excellent; the Dutch Militia were a very good body of men, though young; the Belgians were young and, some of them, very small, but well clothed and equipped and, apparently, well disciplined; the cavalry were well mounted but indifferent riders. In his heart, however, the duke expected little of them, and he would gladly have imported ten thousand of the Portuguese who had fought, generally, well for him in the Peninsula; but his effort to obtain them met with no success. [8]

Altogether the duke was within the bounds of moderation when he described his army as infamous. Nevertheless, though his British troops were for the most part far inferior to any that he had seen in the field since 1794, they, together with the King's German Legion, were his most trustworthy soldiers; and he considered it imperative so to mingle them with the rest as to impart some measure of stability to the whole. In this, however, as in every design which he framed for the organisation and disposition of his forces, he was at the outset thwarted by the King of the Netherlands. This prince was the son of the *stadtholder* who had taken refuge in England in 1795 and had died there in 1806.

Unlike his father, he lacked neither intelligence nor good intentions, and was by no means without experience of military operations in the field. His new position as Sovereign of the Netherlands made, as the British Cabinet recognised, the choice of advisers and administrators very difficult; for he was confronted with the alternatives of employing men of ability and weight but of doubtful loyalty, owing to their former connections, or men of unimpeachable principles but lacking both knowledge and authority. Some of the most important of those whom he actually selected were viewed by Wellington with profound distrust; and to their influence he ascribed the steady opposition of the king to all measures which he recommended.

It is likely enough that the duke was right; for the story of Brit-

---

8. *Wellington Supp. Desp.* 10; and see *Le Bas, La Campagne de 1815, i.*; and James, *Campaign of 1815.* I am afraid that not all the pleading of Le Bas and his collaborator can satisfy me that the Dutch and Belgians were good troops and ready to fight the French. It would be contrary to human nature if they had been; and it is no reproach to them, or at any rate to the Belgians, that they were not.

ish statesmen from 1688 to 1714 and of Napoleon's marshals in 1814 and 1815 shows that, where there are rival dynasties, men generally seek to be on good terms with both. On the other hand, it must be admitted that some of the British demands were calculated to wound the susceptibilities and excite the suspicion of good Netherlander, most notably that which required Ostend and Antwerp, the keys of the British communications, to be entrusted to British commanders. Still, the Dutch had no one but themselves to thank if the Cabinet in Downing Street was wary in dealing with them.

No people could have shown a more wretched spirit in 1793, 1799 and 1814, when the red-coats had landed to help and hearten them to the reconquest of their independence; and too much blood and treasure had already been sacrificed in reliance upon that "rising of the Dutch" which was always promised and never fulfilled. The Hollanders professed to mourn over the freedom of which Napoleon had bereft them; but it was when they thought of their lost commerce that they wailed loudly and from their hearts.

Each party therefore watched carefully for foul dealing in the other; and Wellington, who with all his faults was at least a straightforward man, read treachery in every obstacle raised by the king against his wishes. Perhaps the duke hardly made allowance for the exaltation which kingship might produce upon a potentate who, up to the past twelvemonth, had possessed neither territory nor subjects. A sense of the ridiculous is not too common in royal families. The Prince of Orange had with difficulty been restrained from invading France in order to measure his military genius against Napoleon's; and his father may well have thought that a crown adds an augmentation to the brain as well as an adornment to the brow.

However that may be, the contention between the king and the duke became so hot that Wellington on the 4th of May shook the dust off his feet and sent a message to the effect that, unless His Majesty mended his ways, the British commander would have nothing more to do with him. On the same day the king made over to him with no ill grace the command of the whole of his troops, with the rank of field-marshal in the service of the Netherlands.[9]

This difficulty surmounted, the duke distributed his army into three corps. The First, commanded by the Prince of Orange, consisted of the First and Third British Divisions under Cooke and Charles

---

9. *Wellington Supp. Desp.* 10.

Alten, the 2nd and 3rd Netherlands Divisions under Generals Perponcher and Chassé, and a Dutch division of cavalry under General Collaert. The Second, under Lord Hill (as we must now call him), was made up of the Second and Fourth British Divisions under Clinton and Colville, the 1st Netherlandish Division under General Stedman, and a Netherlandish brigade under General Anthing, the whole of the Netherlanders being subject to Prince Frederick of Orange, aged eighteen.

The Third Corps, or Reserve, was composed of the Fifth and Sixth British Divisions, which were ultimately commanded by Picton and Lambert (for Cole had married a wife and therefore could not come in time for the opening of the campaign), the Nassau contingent of three battalions, the cavalry-divisions of the British and of the King's German Legion (comprehending sixty-nine squadrons in seven brigades, with six batteries of horse-artillery), twelve squadrons of Hanoverian cavalry, and three brigades of Netherlandish cavalry with one battery of horse-artillery. To the Brunswick contingent of eight battalions, four squadrons and two batteries were in due time to be added, for the most part young and raw troops, but steady enough in the cause of the Allies.

But this list by no means exhausts the details of the intermingling. In every British Division except the First, foreigners were blended with red-coats. Alten's and Clinton's had each one brigade of British, one of the Legion, and one of Hanoverians; Picton's and Colville's had each two brigades of British and one of Hanoverians; Lambert's comprised one brigade of British and one of Hanoverians. Even so, however, the subtlety of mixture is not yet wholly expressed. In Cooke's division of Guards the three young battalions were stiffened by one old one from the Peninsula. In Alten's, where all the British were young, the battalions of the Legion were veterans and the Hanoverians were regulars; in Colville's, where the British were both old and young, the Hanoverians were both regulars and Militia; in Clinton's, Picton's and Lambert's, where the British as well as the troops of the Legion were old, the Hanoverians were all Militia. In like manner the Prince of Orange had been careful to mix up regular battalions with Militia and Belgians with Dutch. Well might Wellington doubt the quality of his army and pronounce that its organisation, together with the choice of officers, was a matter of great difficulty.

By extreme good fortune the extension of Prussian territory to the extreme west had brought about the presence of some thirty thousand

Prussian troops and fourteen thousand Saxons, under General Kleist, upon the Lower Rhine. This force was to be completed to five corps with a joint strength of a hundred and twenty thousand men, the whole to be commanded by Blücher, with Gneisenau for the chief of his staff. The number sounded imposing, but the quality of the troops left much to be desired. Nearly half of the infantry—sixty-six out of one hundred and thirty-six battalions—was composed of Militia and, of these sixty-six, twenty-four were of new formation and included six from Westphalia, which had only since the Peace been placed under Prussian rule.

Of the seventy battalions of the Line two were from the Duchy of Berg, the appanage of Murat under Napoleon, and had served in the French Army; and there were among the rest eight thousand recruits levied in the newly acquired provinces between the Rhine and the Meuse. The clothing, equipment and armament of all were equally defective, there being in some regiments muskets of three different calibres, and no uniformity of belts or pouches. The cavalry was in worse condition even than the infantry. The regiments of the Line numbered twenty against fifteen of Militia; but, of the twenty, one half were of recent creation, and, of the fifteen, two had only just been scraped together.

The artillery was well provided with guns but short of gunners—in fact in precisely the same state as the British. Blücher, the commander-in-chief, was a fine fighting soldier, full of activity in spite of his seventy-one years, rough and illiterate but staunch and shrewd, and not in the least afraid of Napoleon. Gneisenau, who was supposed to make good what Blücher lacked in brains, enjoyed a great reputation as a scientific officer and a profound strategist, but did not shine in other capacities, being a timid commander and an indifferent tactician. Unaware of his defects, or at any rate unwilling to admit them, he conceived himself to be undervalued, and vented his spleen in querulousness, jealousy and suspicion; and, though he hated the French, he did not love the English. His talents, however, when added to the peculiar qualities of Blücher, made a very powerful combination.

Let us now turn to Napoleon and take notice of the force that he could match against these two very poor armies of Wellington and Blücher. The France to which he returned was not the France which he had left behind him in 1814; and he presented himself to the nation not as Emperor, but as First Consul, the leader of a revolution which was to overthrow the evils restored by the Bourbons and deliver the people from the tyranny of priests and kings. The remnant of the old revolutionists was inclined to take him at his word and repeat the violence and outrage of 1793; but, once reinstalled at the Tuileries, Napoleon 's innate loathing for the mob reasserted itself, and he began forthwith to resume the pomp and outward trappings of the Empire as if he were once more absolute.

Here, however, he was checked. Moderate as well as extreme men exclaimed against a despotism and clamoured for a liberal constitution; and, unless he were prepared to make himself a mere chief of revolutionary *banditti*, he was bound to give way. In truth his return was not very welcome except to his old companions in arms. The heads of the provincial administration, though half of them had been nominated by him and continued in their places by the Bourbons, showed no zeal in his cause. Their underlings were actively unfriendly; and an attempt to get rid of them by a new election had no effect but to reinstate them with greater influence. The permanent civil service contained many adherents of King Louis. The clergy were naturally irreconcilably hostile.

In La Vendee there was from the end of April a renewal of insurrection. Everywhere it was realised that the Empire signified war, whereas the entire nation longed for peace. The funds, having fallen with a rush from 78 to 58 within less than a month, continued to sink slowly through May and June; and no efforts of Napoleon could arrest them. He quickly produced a constitution, more liberal than that granted by the Bourbons, which bewildered many and pleased none; and he appointed the 1st of June for its solemn ratification by the people.

Even in dealing with the troops he was cautious of exercising arbitrary power. The Army of Louis the Eighteenth numbered slightly over two hundred thousand men, but Napoleon dared not double its strength by such measures as had been the rule under the Empire. There were something over one hundred thousand more men who were on leave or who had taken leave, or, in plain English, deserted; and it was reckoned that sixty thousand of these could be recovered.

The emperor, however, delayed to call them to the colours until he had sent a circular to the powers of Europe making proposals for a peaceful settlement. This missive was returned unopened by the Prince Regent of England and rejected with as little ceremony by the rest. The summons was meanwhile issued, and seventy-five thousand men responded to the call. Voluntary enlistment produced fifteen thousand more, and the enrolment of the seamen at the national dockyards added yet another six thousand.

At the end of June, moreover, Napoleon hardened his heart to conscribe the men due for service in 1815, some of whom had already served under him in 1814; and within a week nearly fifty thousand of them were assembled in the various departmental centres. Besides these there were at his disposal the National Guard, consisting of some two hundred thousand men between the ages of twenty and sixty, and capable of expansion to more than ten times that number. Of these he ordered for the present the mobilisation of some two hundred and thirty thousand; and, notwithstanding recalcitrance in some quarters, one hundred and fifty thousand were at their appointed stations, in fortress or in camp, by the second week of June. With them, five and twenty thousand veterans and sundry local corps sufficed for the guarding of strong places and frontier-roads.

Thus there was a fair prospect that half a million French would be more or less ready for the field by August; but small arms and cartridges were scarce and, though there was abundance of cannon, carriages and ammunition were deficient. Moreover the magazines were empty, the clothing of the existing troops was in rags, and both cavalry and artillery were very short of horses. With his usual energy and resource the emperor set himself to remedy these defects and to repair the fortifications; and being ably seconded by Davoût, whom he had placed in charge of the Ministry of War, he achieved an astonishing measure of success.

The order for mobilisation had hardly been issued before the indefatigable brain had sketched the organisation of the force, which was altered at the end of May into its final form—an Army of the North, one hundred and twenty-four thousand men, under Napoleon's own command; an Army of the Rhine, twenty thousand men, under Rapp; another of the Alps, twenty-four thousand men under Suchet, with subsidiary corps, amounting together to fourteen thousand men, in support; and two corps of the Eastern and Western Pyrenees, fourteen thousand men, under Decaen and Clausel.

The greater number of his generals rallied to him; but a few stood aloof, and a few more, though willing, were rejected. Of the marshals, Victor, Marmont and Berthier, who had followed Louis to Belgium, were struck off the list, and Augereau with them. Oudinot, Gouvion St. Cyr, and Kellermann were left severely alone; Masséna and Macdonald were pressed to accept commands but refused them. Berthier, who was at Bamberg when Napoleon left Elba, was anxious to return to France, but was denied a passport. On the 1st of June he fell, apparently by accident, from a window on the third floor of his house to the pavement below, and was picked up dead. Soult, therefore, was installed as Chief of the Staff, a position for which his great military talents, impaired as they were only by his irresolution on the battlefield, seemed particularly to qualify him.

In the Army of the North, which was distributed into five corps, the generals of Spain were again prominent, the first corps being assigned to d'Erlon and the second to Reille. The three that remained were allotted to Vandamme, Gérard and Mouton, Count Lobau. Drouot took charge of the Imperial Guard and Grouchy of the cavalry.

There is still a name wanting from the list of Napoleon's greatest lieutenants, that of Joachim Murat, King of Naples. On the eve of his escape from Elba Napoleon had sent him a message, bidding him prepare for war, since, if the Austrians declared against the revival of the French Empire, the Neapolitan army would be required for an important diversion against them. At the outset Murat declared to the ministers at Vienna that his policy should be subordinated to that of the Emperor Francis; but, fearing lest Napoleon might re-annex Italy, he prepared to conquer Italy for himself.

On the 29th of March he moved his army from Ancona towards Bologna. Then crossing the line of demarcation between Austrian and Italian territory, he advanced to Rimini, and on the 30th published a proclamation calling all Italians to arms for the freedom and unity of their country. Advancing next to Bologna, from which the Austrians fell back before him, he on the 4th of April occupied Ferrara, Modena and Florence. There his progress was stayed. The Austrians, having gathered in force behind the Po, repelled all his efforts to cross the river, and taking the offensive thrust him back to Ancona. The decisive battle was fought on the 2nd and 3rd of May, which left him a week later with only ten thousand of the forty thousand men with which he had begun the campaign.

On the 19th he fled from Naples to Toulon, from whence he sent a letter to Napoleon asking for a command in his army. Napoleon, sufficiently vexed that his only ally in Europe should have spent his strength in a mad enterprise which could profit no one except his enemies, rejected the overture in harsh terms; and therewith vanished all hope that Murat would take his old place at the head of the French cavalry.

Various plans of campaign were produced from the various capitals of the powers, but were finally reduced by Schwarzenberg to one. According to this, France was to be invaded by six armies simultaneously. On the extreme right, that is to say in the north, Wellington with ninety to a hundred thousand men was to advance between Maubeuge and Beaumont; on the left of Wellington the Prussians under Blücher, rather under one hundred and twenty thousand men, were to penetrate between Philippeville and Givet; on the left of Blücher one hundred and fifty thousand Russians under Barclay de Tolly were to enter by Sarrelouis and Saarbrück; and on the left of de Tolly two hundred thousand Austrians and South Germans were to break in by Sarreguemines and Bâle; and the whole of them were to converge by Péronne, Laon, Nancy and Langres upon Paris.

On the extreme south fifty thousand Austrians and Piedmontese from Upper Italy, and twenty-five thousand more Austrians, who were opposed to Murat, were to cross the Alps and turn right and left upon Lyon and Provence. In their usual leisurely fashion the Austrians set down the opening of the campaign for the end of June or beginning of July, since they and the Russians could not count upon being complete and in readiness at an earlier date. Meanwhile, of course, the armies of Wellington and Blücher were to form the outposts of the entire host, so as to cover the general concentration on the eastern frontier of France.

Wellington, and for that matter Blücher also, were strongly opposed to delay and anxious to take the offensive as soon as possible, so as to check, or at any rate to embarrass, the re-establishment of Napoleon's authority by showing the French people the disastrous consequence of accepting it. Wellington also insisted particularly upon the importance of preventing Napoleon from gathering any headway outside the boundaries of France. The great emperor's system was, so far as possible, to support his armies at the expense of his enemies, to make war, as Wellington put it, a pecuniary resource; and the duke had truly foretold in the Peninsula that, as soon as hostilities were transferred to the soil of France, the zeal of the French soldiers and inhabitants would very quickly languish.

Again, a triumphal entry, bloodless or the reverse, into Belgium, would certainly rally the Belgians, and probably the Dutch also, to Napoleon; and the moral effect in Europe would be very great. The new King of the Netherlands had just set up his capital at Brussels. The restored King of France had taken refuge at Ghent. If both of these potentates were forced to take to their heels because the Allies from want of energy or alleged military reasons were unable to protect them, the old legend of Napoleon's invincibility would be re-established and his partisans would show their heads all over Europe.

In England, for instance—and this was what Wellington particularly dreaded—the existing Ministry might be driven from office with the full assent of their former supporters, now become "peace-mad," and would be replaced by such men as Grey, Whitbread and Tierney, hungry for office after twenty years of exclusion, strongly possessed by the false beliefs which they had been proclaiming for years, and practically committed to a reversal of the government's policy, not because it was wrong but because it was the government's.

If England withdrew from the Coalition, all resistance to Napoleon was at an end, for without England's subsidies the remaining powers could not keep their armies in the field, and the emperor might resume his sway in Europe as early as he pleased. It was in this light that the coming campaign presented itself to Wellington. Now, more even than in the worst days of the Peninsular War, the existing ministry depended upon him whether it should stand or fall; and upon the maintenance of the mnistry depended the defeat of Napoleon.

A short semblance of success on the part of the enemy might suffice to bring about the great disaster. It may seem almost incredible that a few factious utterances by a handful of mediocre men—utterances inspired rather by vanity, by the habit of contention and the excitement of rhetorical combat than by any sincere desire to do mischief—should cramp the movements and vitiate the dispositions of a great commander in the field; but undoubtedly they did so in 1815; and the consequences were likely to have been the more serious because the commander was, as he truly said, at the head of an infamous army.

CHAPTER 2

The Armies March

As a matter of fact Napoleon could have invaded Belgium with every chance of success at the end of March, 1815. Kleist and the Prince of Orange could not have raised, between them, more than eighty thousand men, of which number twenty-four thousand Saxons and Netherlanders were not to be trusted, and the remainder were mostly half-trained troops. Against them Napoleon could have pitted fifty thousand seasoned soldiers, and, encountering such commanders, could hardly have failed of a great initial success. The prince and Kleist were prepared for such a movement, but could not agree where to meet it.

The Prince of Orange, in his anxiety to take the offensive, had disposed his troops upon a line running from Tournai through Ath and along the course of the Sambre to Namur, where was stationed the Prussian vanguard; and he was anxious to give battle on the south side of Brussels. Kleist, on the other hand, fearing for his communications, held the maintenance of the line of the Meuse to be the most important object. As a matter of strategic principle Sir Hudson Lowe agreed with Kleist, but considered that strategic considerations were overruled by the political inexpediency of throwing the entire country south of Brussels, already not too well affected towards the new King of the Netherlands, into the arms of Napoleon.

Kleist and the prince accordingly compromised their difference by arranging that, in case of an attack, the prince's own army should retire while Kleist's should advance, and that their united forces should give battle at Tirlemont, about thirteen miles east of Brussels.

Wellington, as may be supposed, settled the question immediately after his arrival by advocating that the Prussian Army and his own should unite at once south of Brussels, rather than allow the French to

BELGIUM
and
PART OF FRANCE
to illustrate the
CAMPAIGN OF 1815
English Miles

Flushing

Ostend

Bruges

B

Nieuport

Ghent

E

Calais

Gravelines

Dunkirk

Alost

Ypres

Audenarde

Courtrai

Renaix

Boulogne

St Omer

Roubaix

Leuze

R. Lys

Lille

Tournai

Mons

C

Montreuil

Lens

St Amand

Valenciennes

Douay

R. Canche

F

Arras

Maubeuge

Cambrai

Lequesnoy

Abbeville

Landrecies

R. Somme

R. Breslc

R

Amiens

Peronne

St Quentin

R. Oise

A

Laon

R. Serre

Beauvais

Compiègne

Soissons

R. Aisne

R. Oise

Longitude East

O L L A N D

Antwerp

Liers

Malines

Louvain

BRUSSELS

Waterloo   Wavre

Genappe

G

Charleroi

Namur   Huy

Tirlemont   Loetz   Maastricht

Trond

Hannut   Waremme

Tongres

Liège

Verviers

Aix la Chapelle

Crefeld

Düsseldorf

R. Rhine

To Cologne

51

G   E   R   M   A   N   Y

L   U   M   B   U   R   G

Ciney

Dinant   Marche

Rochefort

Philippeville

Beaumont

Charleville

Mézières

Sedan

R. Meuse

Chum

Montmédy   Longwy

LUXEMBURG

Luxemburg

Treves

Thionville

50

d e n n e s

N   C   E

Greenwich

5   6

be in possession of the Belgian capital even for a moment. The question was no easy one of solution. The Prussian communications lay towards the east, the British towards the west, the Dutch towards the north. Which of them was to sacrifice its line of operations in case of mishap? Without immediately raising this issue, Gneisenau consented to move Prussian troops farther westward so that the most advanced of them should occupy Charleroi and the ground west of it so far as the Roman road from Binche to Bavai, but asked for further light upon Wellington's plans.

The duke in reply admitted that political considerations counted for much in the disposition which he advocated, and conceded further that to allow them too much weight, as compared with purely military exigencies, was as great a blunder as the converse. He then gave it as his opinion that, if Napoleon should advance, he would probably choose the line between the Scheldt and the Sambre, or in other words that he would strike at the British communications. In that case the Prussians at Charleroi would form the left of the line, the rest of the Prussians being concentrated at Namur. Battle would then be offered south of Brussels, and, in case of mishap, the entire army would retreat upon Liége and Maastricht or even, if necessary, still farther east to Juliers.

This signified plainly that, if circumstances should demand it, the British and Dutch would abandon their communications and shift their line of operation eastward. Gneisenau, emphasising this point, declared that all difficulties were now at an end, and that he accepted Wellington's plan without hesitation. Wellington rejoined that only the peculiarity of the circumstances could warrant him in thus giving up his connection with the sea; but that any retreat of the Allies could at worst be but momentary—indeed they were already in too great strength to think of retreat or even of being attacked. [1] This last opinion, written on the 13th of April, referred of course only to the situation of the moment and signified no more than that a raid from Napoleon with a small force, for the sake of rallying the Belgians to his standard, was now out of the question.

On the other hand the collapse of the Duke of Angoulême's operations forbade an early offensive of the Allies such as Wellington had hoped to undertake in support of the royalists in France. The British commander now turned his attention rather to the defence of the Low Countries, hastening the repair of the fortresses in West

---

1. *Wellington Desp.* to Gneisenau; to Clancarty, *Supp. Desp.* 10.

Flanders within the quadrilateral Ostend, Ypres, Mons, Antwerp, and offering to supply twelve thousand of the twenty-seven thousand men required for their garrisons from his British and Hanoverian infantry. On the 21st of April Blücher arrived at Liége, upon which point the Prussian Army was rapidly assembling; and Wellington, bidding him welcome, sent Colonel Henry Hardinge as British *attaché* to the Prussian headquarters.

Throughout this time an infinity of business was pressed upon Wellington. There were long letters as to the attitude of Spain, equally long letters as to the prospects of obtaining a contingent from Portugal, constant references to the business transacted, or untransacted, at Vienna, the soreness of Prussia at being restrained from swallowing up Saxony, the allotment of the German contingents to the armies of Blücher and of the duke himself, the arrangements for the subsistence, upon Netherlandish territory, of the Prussian armies, which as usual were extremely arbitrary and rapacious, above all the distribution of the subsidies to hungry and impecunious powers, whose representatives vied with each other in parading the sacrifices and poverty of their nations. Everything was thrown upon him; and, as holder in some degree of the English purse-strings, he was treated by his German colleagues of all professions, Blücher perhaps excepted, with a kind of jealous servility. It was no easy course that was given him to steer; and indeed his functions during this campaign, as in the Peninsula, were perhaps even more diplomatic than military.

In the matter of his relations with the Prussians there were two initial difficulties. First, the Prussian Army was divided into rival parties, headed by Generals Knesebeck and Gneisenau; and, since Knesebeck for his own ends favoured close joint action between the British and Prussians, it was natural that Gneisenau should cherish a contrary view. In the second place, Wellington's feelings towards France were widely different from the Prussian. Gneisenau not unnaturally, considering all that his adopted country had suffered at the hands of the French armies, was for making the war one of punishment for the French nation, and a means of "humbling their military spirit."

Wellington wished only to get rid of Napoleon, and to spare the French as much as possible. It was thus that he had rendered the approach of the red-coats more welcome than that of Soult's soldiers to the inhabitants of Southern France. Some substitute for Napoleon must, however, be found, and Wellington agreed with Castlereagh in thinking that the restoration of Louis the Eighteenth would be the most certain means of assuring the tranquillity of Europe for a short time. But all reports from France were so unfavourable to this solution, and the Tsar Alexander was known to be so adverse to it, that Wellington, while still working for it, thought success almost impossible of attainment. [2]

All through April British reinforcements continued slowly to trickle over to Flanders, and at the end of the month Lord Uxbridge arrived to take command of the cavalry. On the 1st of May there was an alarm of an attack, and Wellington issued alternative orders for a concentration of the British and Netherlandish armies to meet a French advance either between the Lys and the Scheldt or between the Scheldt and the Sambre.

In the first case the inundations about Oudenarde and Ghent were to be let loose; and the British were to concentrate between the Scheldt and the Sambre in readiness to cross the former river, while the Netherlanders were to assemble at Soignies and Nivelles. In the second event both British and Netherlanders were to be gathered together at Enghien and Soignies. The intent was very evidently to cover Ghent and Brussels, the temporary home of King Louis and the newly established capital of King William.

On the 3rd of May Wellington rode over to Tirlemont to meet Blücher, with whom he had a conversation which he described as very satisfactory, the purport of it being, apparently, that Blücher had promised to stand by him and not allow him to be overwhelmed by superior numbers. Since the armies of the two marshals combined amounted to one hundred and fifty thousand men, and Napoleon's, by all reports, did not exceed one hundred and fifteen thousand, Wellington had hopes of "giving a good account even of Bonaparte." [3]

The alarm passed off, and the next incident was a mutiny of Blücher's fourteen thousand Saxon troops, which compelled their removal from the fighting line to the rear. This was no very great matter, for the loyalty of these Saxons had always been doubtful, and it was better that they should declare themselves at a safe moment than in the middle of active operations; but it is significant that the King of Saxony entreated Wellington to take them under his command, [4] attributing their misconduct entirely to rude handling on the part of the Prussians, and

2. *Wellington Supp. Desp.* 10.
3. *Wellington Desp.* Memo, from the Prince of Orange, 1st May. To Prince of Orange and Hardenberg, 3rd May 1815.
4. *Supp. Desp.* 10.

engaging to answer for their fidelity if subjected to the duke.

In the course of the month the English battalions promised to Wellington commenced to cross the Channel in driblets, and he began to chafe at the delay in opening the campaign. He had fairly good intelligence of the strength of the enemy from Clarke, Napoleon's late Minister of War, who was now with Louis the Eighteenth at Ghent; and he was satisfied that the British and Prussians could not move until the main body of the Allies should come up; but none the less he had an uneasy feeling that every day gained by Napoleon was to the advantage of the enemy. Intelligence from the frontier continued to be contradictory. On the 8th of May the duke wrote that he and Blücher were so well united and so strong that he had little apprehension of an attack.

On the 9th, upon the news of a French concentration at Valenciennes and Maubeuge, he was inclined to contract his cantonments a little. A few days later there were signs that the enemy contemplated a defensive rather than an offensive campaign; but, in accordance with concerted arrangements, the Prussians drew a little closer to the British, and on the 11th of May Blücher fixed his headquarters at Hannut, about twenty miles west of Liége. Still the prevailing impression both at the British and the Prussian headquarters was that their armies were doomed to a tedious series of sieges of the French fortresses on the frontier; and Gneisenau was inclined to think that the operations would require five hundred siege-cannon.[5]

On the 22nd of May French patrols encountered the Prince of Orange's outposts, a little to the east and to the south of Mons, and fired the first shots of the campaign; but the incident was of no importance. On the 21st Wellington announced that, though still without some of the German contingents that had been promised to him, he could, after making provision for all garrisons, take the field with seventy-six thousand bayonets and sabres;[6] and on the 30th he wrote to Uxbridge that there was a prospect of moving shortly.[7] Blücher was impatient to open the campaign; and it was hoped that, upon the arrival of the Austrians on the Rhine at about the middle of June, the entire force under the Prince and Wellington would advance in earnest.[8]

In the first days of June there were again reports of a French con-

---

5. *Supp. Desp.* 10.
6. *Wellington Desp.* To Schwartzenberg, 21st May 1815.
7. *Ibid.* To Uxbridge, 1st June 1815.
8. *Ibid.* To H. Wellesley, 2nd June 1815.

centration at Maubeuge, and Wellington on the 7th issued his final orders as to the defence of the fortresses of Western Flanders. [9] French newspapers, carefully falsified, announced that Napoleon would leave Paris for Laon on the 6th. Another report [10] said that he would go to Douai on the same day, would make a false attack on the Prussians and a real attack on the English, and destroy both before the Russians came up. The air was full of rumours and contradictions; and Napoleon was reported to be at half a dozen different places before he had ever left Paris. On the 10th Clarke sent a final estimate of the strength and distribution of the French force, reckoning the troops at Napoleon's disposal in the north very correctly at one hundred and twenty thousand men.

On the 11th a Colonel Dillon of the British Army arrived at Mons, and gave it as certain intelligence that Napoleon had reached Avesnes. On the 12th five deserters came into Mons from Landrecies with information that Napoleon was just come to Laon. Other intelligencers brought news that Reille's corps had reached Maubeuge; that a division of the Imperial Guard was due to arrive at Avesnes, to which place headquarters would be transferred immediately, and that Soult had passed through Valenciennes and Maubeuge, *incognito*, also on his way to Avesnes. [11] On the 13th there were reports from more than one source of a French concentration at Maubeuge; and on the 14th the troops at Maubeuge were stated to be moving eastward upon Beaumont.

Early in the afternoon General Dörnberg wrote to headquarters that, according to the latest accounts, there were one hundred thousand men between Maubeuge and Philippeville; and Hardinge at ten o'clock of the same night announced that at the Prussian headquarters a French attack was expected, and that some preliminary orders had been given tending towards the concentration of the Prussian army to meet it. Nevertheless the Allied armies both of Wellington and Blücher remained in their original cantonments, which, as shall now be shown, were of dangerous extension.

On the right or west of the line the headquarters of Hill's, the Second Corps, were at Ath. Of his two British divisions, Colville's headquarters were at Oudenarde; the division being thrown back more or less *en potence*, with one of its Hanoverian brigades at Nieuport,

9. *Ibid.* To Prince of Orange, 7th June 1815. *Supp. Desp.* 10.
10. *Supp. Desp.* 10.
11. *Ibid.*

Mitchell's brigade about Renaix, and Johnstone's between Courtrai and Oudenarde. Clinton's headquarters were at Ath, where was stationed Du Plat's brigade of the German Legion; the Fifty-second and a Hanoverian brigade being posted between the town and Lessines, with the remainder of Adam's brigade at Leuze. Next to these, east of Colville and north of Clinton, were Stedman's Netherlandish division, with headquarters at Sotteghem, cantonments scattered between that village and Ghent, and Anthing's Dutch brigade still farther north at Alost.

The First Army Corps, under the Prince of Orange, had its headquarters at Braine-le-Comte. Of Cooke's British division the Guards were at Enghien and Byng's brigade at the village of Marcq, practically touching the Guards. The headquarters of Alten's division were at Soignies; Colin Halkett's brigade had been distributed south-westward of it as far as Lens, Kielmansegge's Hanoverians a little to south of Halkett, and Ompteda's north-westward towards Ath. Farther east, Chassé's Netherlandish division, with headquarters at Roeulx, was disposed southward towards Binche, and Perponcher's, with headquarters at Nivelles, reached as far south-eastward as Frasnes and Villers Perwin. The Reserve was assembled in and about Brussels.

The British and Hanoverian cavalry were distributed along the line of the Haine from Mons by Jemappes, St. Ghislain, Roucourt and Béclers to Tournai and Menin, with two regiments at Ghent, and a brigade between Ninove and Grammont, at which last place were Uxbridge's head quarters. General Dörnberg, who commanded the 3rd Brigade, was stationed at Mons and charged with the collection of intelligence from the frontier. Eastward from Mons the Netherlandish cavalry watched the frontier as far as Binche, from which point, or rather from Bonne Esperance, a little farther south, they were relieved by the Prussians.

The 1st Prussian Corps, under Ziethen, had its headquarters at Charleroi and extended from Fontaine l'Évêque on the west through Marchienne to Moustier on the east, its reserves of infantry being at Fleurus, of cavalry at Sombreffe, and of artillery at Gembloux. Its outposts ran from Bonne Esperance, south-eastward through Thuin and Gerpinnes to Sosoye, a total front of close on thirty miles.

On Ziethen's left the IInd Corps, under General von Pirch I., [12] had its headquarters and one brigade at Namur, another parallel to it

12. There was a second General von Pirch in command of a brigade of Ziethen's corps, who is distinguished as Pirch II.

on the Meuse at Huy, a third midway between them to the north at Heron, the fourth at Thorombais-les-Béguignes, eighteen miles due north of Namur, the reserve infantry on the road between these two places, and the reserve artillery at Hannut.

The IIIrd Corps had its headquarters and one brigade at Ciney, about fifteen miles south-east of Namur; the reserve artillery lay on the road to Namur, with a second brigade of foot north-west of it at Assesse, and the reserve cavalry on the road to Dinant, where there was a third brigade of infantry. The fourth brigade of infantry lay at Huy.

Of the IVth Corps one brigade was with headquarters at Liége; another a little to the north at Liers, with the reserve cavalry and artillery a short distance to north-east of it; a third brigade lay five miles to west of Liége at Hollogne-aux-Pierres, and the fourth still farther to west at Waremme.

The shape of the line thus held from Ostend through Tournai and Mons to Liége was convex, and in its full extent about one hundred and fifty miles, of which, roughly speaking, one hundred miles were guarded by the hundred and five thousand men under Wellington and fifty by the hundred and twenty thousand men of Blücher. The headquarters of the two chiefs, Brussels and Namur, were thirty-two miles apart by road. Taking Nivelles, immediately to north of Fontaine l'Évêque, as the point of junction between the two armies, the remotest of the Prussians at Liége and of the British at Oudenarde could not possibly have reached it in less than two days. This dispersion was explained by Wellington, so far as his army was concerned, by the imperative necessity for watching the four great roads that led from Lille, Condé, and Valenciennes upon Ghent and Brussels.

It was on one or other of these lines, it must be repeated, that he looked for an attack, if any should be delivered. He had therefore arranged his dispositions to concentrate either to west or to south; he had made fortified passages over the rivers; and he had repaired the fortresses of Nieuport, Ostend, Ypres, Menin, Courtrai, Oudenarde, Tournai, Ath and Mons, so as to place the weakest of them beyond reach of a stroke of surprise, and to make the strongest of them defy any onslaught less formidable than a regular siege. A hostile concentration at Maubeuge in itself by no means belied his prevision, for the enemy might advance from thence as readily upon Mons as upon Charleroi or any other point upon the Sambre. Assuming then that he had rightly divined his enemy's purpose, which the event showed that he had not, his arrangements were intelligible.

The like can hardly be said of the Prussians. The dissemination of their army was excused upon the ground that, if the cantonments were contracted, the victualling of the force became impossible. There was no doubt some truth in this; though it seems that the difficulty was greatly of the Prussian's own making, for they deliberately imported dissension into the ranks of the Allies by endeavouring to take their subsistence by force from the Netherlander instead of paying for it. [13] But in any case the disposition of the IIIrd Corps within the triangle between Namur, Huy and Dinant, facing west, seems to be absolutely meaningless as a defensive measure; and, as Wellington pointed out, pending the arrival of the Austrians and Russians, the attitude of the Allied armies in the Low Countries was inevitably defensive.

If any French offensive movement were apprehended from Philippeville, a small corps of cavalry would have sufficed to watch Dinant and the line of the Meuse southward from Namur. If again Gneisenau dreaded a blow at his communications, after the manner of Saxe and Carnot, the obvious precaution was to shift his line of operations from Liége and Namur to the great Roman road, which runs through Tongres to Maastricht, and to have moved the IIIrd and IVth Corps farther to the north. But he, even as Wellington, thought his own army too strong to be attacked; and the arrangements of both were made rather for the coming invasion of France than for the defence of the Low Countries.

Still more curious were Gneisenau's orders and measures in case of an attack on the line of the Sambre. There were bridges at Lobbes, Thuin, Abbaye d'Aulne, Marchienne, Charleroi and Chatelet, all of which lay within the sphere of observation of Ziethen's corps. No attempt was made to prepare these for demolition; indeed the bare fact that they were of masonry was accepted in the Prussian army as warrant that they were indestructible. Further, orders were issued by Gneisenau that no gun was to be unlimbered on the bridges, and that their defence was to be limited to a powerful fire of skirmishers. At this rate it is difficult to understand why the Prussian General went through the form of stationing three brigades of infantry on the river at all; for a few vedettes might perfectly well have watched the points of passage if there were no intention to defend them.

But it is fairly evident that Gneisenau still cherished a predilection

---

13. This gave Wellington much trouble. See *Despatches*. To Clancarty, 14th May; to Hardinge, 24th May 1815. *Supp. Desp.* 10.

for the cordon-system which had ruined the Austrian campaign of the Low Countries in 1793 and 1794. However, Ziethen's instructions were, in case he were assailed in force, to abandon the whole of the ground that he had been watching from Bonne Esperance to Châtelet and to concentrate at Fleurus; which meant that he was to retire to a flank, leaving a gap of over fifteen miles in the Allied line from Binche to beyond Charleroi, and uncovering the direct road from Charleroi to Brussels by Quatre-Bras.

One wonders whether this was part of the "satisfactory" arrangement agreed to between Blücher and Wellington. The duke had freely offered, in case of a reverse, to abandon his line of communication with the sea and to retreat eastward; and upon this understanding Gneisenau had consented to bring his army forward and help Wellington to keep the enemy, if possible, out of Belgium. But, if at the first serious thrust at its line of outposts the Prussian advanced corps were to shrink away to eastward and throw open the direct road to Brussels, then obviously Wellington must either conform to the movement, making a flank march across the front of the assailing army, or retire northward, if not westward, and be wholly separated from Blücher. The neglect of this important point seems to reflect no great credit upon the foresight of either commander.

Such was the situation when cumulative intelligence of the assembly of the French about Maubeuge, Beaumont and Philippeville caused Gneisenau at noon of the 14th to order Thielmann and Bülow to contract the cantonments of the Prussian IIIrd and IVth Corps. Further information received later in the day prompted him, [14] shortly before midnight, to send further and more definite instructions with a view to the concentration of the entire army. Thielmann was to leave small detachments to watch Dinant and the approaches to Givet, and bring the rest of his force to the left bank of the Meuse about Namur; Pirch I. was to collect the IInd Corps between Namur and Fleurus at Mazy and Onoz; and Bülow was politely requested to gather the IVth Corps about Hannut on the 15th and to fix his headquarters there. But no hint was given to Bülow that this movement was to be part of a general concentration; and not a word was sent to Wellington to inform him that such a concentration had even been thought of.

Meanwhile Napoleon had been laying his plans with his best skill. He had early resolved to take the offensive, and to assail the Allies in Flanders, hoping that, by beating Blücher's and Wellington's armies in

---

14. Blücher was asleep, so Gneisenau took the duty upon himself

turn, he would rally all Belgium to his standard, bring a peace-loving ministry into power at Downing Street, and be free to march with his victorious army to the Vosges to throw back the Austrians and Prussians. It was open to him to strike at the Allies by their right flank, their left flank, or their centre. He rejected the first and second plans because, in addition to incidental objections, the turning of either flank would drive the British to unite with the Prussians, or the Prussians to unite with the British, whereas his purpose was to keep them apart and if possible to defeat them piecemeal.

He considered that nothing less than a victory would drive the British Ministers from power, whereas Wellington, who was the better judge on such a point, conceived that the occupation of even half of Belgium would suffice; and therein lies the root of the difference of opinion between them, which reacted so powerfully upon the conduct of the campaign. Napoleon therefore decided to fall upon the armies of Blücher and Wellington at their point of junction with all possible secrecy and swiftness.

At the beginning of June the five corps of the Army of the North were posted about Lille, Valenciennes, Mezières, Thionville and Soissons, with the Imperial Guard at Paris, and the Reserve Cavalry between the Aisne and the Sambre. Screened by the fortresses on the frontier and by the belt of forest that extends from Thuin almost to Namur on the south of the Sambre, the concentration of these forces was to such a master of the art no difficult matter, and was rendered the easier by the unwillingness of the Allies to send even the smallest military bodies across the frontier. The Imperial Guard were the first to move, marching in detachments between the 5th and the 8th of June upon Avesnes by way of Soissons; Gérard with the 4th Corps was the next, leaving Metz on the 6th for Philippeville; d'Erlon quitted Lille on the 9th for Valenciennes, from which Reille moved out at his approach, and the two marched eastward upon Maubeuge.

Vandamme shifted from Mezières to Philippeville, and the rest of the troops were directed to Beaumont. Napoleon himself left Paris early on the 12th, breakfasted at Soissons, slept at Laon, and arrived at Avesnes on the 13th. By the night of the 14th the whole were assembled on a line of about sixteen miles between Solre-sur-Sambre and Philippeville. The entire manoeuvre was conducted with the strictest secrecy; all communication with Belgium and the Rhine provinces was closed; an embargo was laid on all ships even to the very fishing-boats; and at every point from which regular troops had been withdrawn, National Guards were pushed up to take their place. Only one small detail went amiss. Soult omitted to send the requisite orders to Grouchy for the march of the cavalry, and it was only upon Napoleon's arrival at Laon, where were Grouchy's headquarters, that the mistake was corrected. Even so the whole of the horse arrived at Avesnes on the night of the 13th, though not without forced marches exhausting to both beasts and men.

Thus the information which had reached the Allied commanders on the 12th, 13th and 14th was in the main correct. The movements of the Guard, of d'Erlon and Reille were accurately given, and the progress of Soult, *incognito*, was truly reported. It must, however, be said for Wellington and Blücher that marches and counter-marches of French troops upon the northern frontier had for weeks been incessant, and that, until the very end, any attempt to piece them together as an indication of the enemy's plans was hopeless. Both of the Allied Commanders have been reproached for not making greater use of their cavalry to penetrate Napoleon's intentions; but it seems to be literally true that both of them, and not Wellington only, were embarrassed by uncertainty whether they were at war or at peace.

Bülow pleaded his ignorance of the fact, that there had been no declaration of war, in excuse for the slowness of his movements, shortly to be narrated, on the 15th of June. Napoleon himself on the 7th of June denounced the action of England in capturing a French frigate in the Mediterranean, as "bloodshed during peace"; and, as if conscious that the signal for opening the war lay with himself, he wrote definitely to Davoût on the 11th of June that hostilities would begin on the 14th. This peculiarity of the situation has, as it seems to me, escaped the notice of most of the later writers upon the campaign of 1815.

It is urged by at least one of them that the manifesto of the Allied Powers of the 13th of March was in itself a declaration of war; but it was rather a decree of outlawry against an individual whose authority as ruler of France was expressly set aside. The document certainly implied that those who followed Napoleon's banner would do so at their peril; but beyond question, if the Allies had invaded France before Napoleon attacked them, they would have issued a proclamation calling upon all Frenchmen to dissociate themselves from him and promising them good treatment if they should do so.

The Powers of Europe were dealing, as they well knew, with a military revolt, not with a national movement; and it would have been impolitic as well as contrary to their professions to treat the French nation as if it were the French Army. On the other hand, it may justly be argued that, given such a state of uncertainty and the presence of a French host under Napoleon, the utmost care should have been taken that everything should be ready against a sudden attack. On the contrary, both Blücher and Wellington were so confident of their superiority that they took less instead of more than the ordinary precautions, feeling sure that Napoleon would not venture upon an offensive movement. They were wrong in their divination of his intentions; but their trust in their own strength was justified by the result. [15]

On the 14th, the anniversary of Marengo and Friedland, Napoleon issued the last of those stirring appeals which had so often stimulated his armies to victory, and in the evening dictated his justly famous orders for the movements of the morrow. The army was to advance upon Charleroi in three principal columns; Reille's and d'Erlon's corps on the left by Thuin and Marchienne; Vandamme's and Lobau's corps, the Imperial Guard and Grouchy's reserve of cavalry in the centre by Ham-sur-Heure and Marcinelle; Gérard's corps by Florennes and Gerpinnes. The whole were to be covered by a screen of cavalry from the centre column and headed by Domont's three regiments of mounted chasseurs, with Pajol's corps of six more regiments of light horse and two battalions of horse-artillery in support. Domont was to start at half-past two in the morning, Pajol and the heads of the infantry at three o'clock; the foot taking the main roads and the horse the by-roads.

Reille, Vandamme, Pajol and Gérard were to keep themselves in constant communication with each other so as to arrive in one united mass before Charleroi. In the centre column the 3rd Corps was to take the lead, to be followed by the 6th Corps at four o'clock and by the various sections of the Guard at half-hourly intervals between five and six. The pontoon-train was to provide three sections to throw as many bridges over the Sambre, which the Emperor intended to cross with his whole army before noon, he himself accompanying the advanced guard of the centre column. For the general purposes of the campaign he designed to divide his army into two wings and a reserve, the left wing under Ney, who was on the point of joining him, the right under Grouchy, and the reserve, which would be strengthened from one wing or the other, according to circumstances, under his personal command.

---

15. *Carres, de Napoléon*, 22023, 22040. Pollio, *Waterloo* (French translation), 101, 129 *n.*

At half-past three in the morning of the 15th the French vanguards crossed the Netherlandish frontier at Leers, Cour-sur-Heure and Thy-le-Chateau; but whether from neglect on the part of the staff or indolence on the part of the generals, there was delay in the march of the rear of the columns. D'Erlon did not set the 1st Corps in motion until half-past four, instead of at three, as he had been bidden. The officer who was carrying the orders to Vandamme was disabled through a fall from his horse; and, as Soult sent no second messenger, Vandamme had no knowledge of the intended movement until Lobau's corps came up to his bivouac. The 4th Corps, which should have marched from Philippeville at three, did not reach Florennes—a distance of not more than five miles—until seven o'clock, and was there bewildered and dismayed by the desertion to the Allies of one of its divisional generals, Bourmont, together with the whole of his staff.

However, the advanced parties on the French centre and left in due time came into collision with the outposts of Pirch I.'s brigade, and pressed them slowly back from position to position until between nine and ten o'clock they reached the Sambre at Marchienne and Charleroi, and found the bridges barricaded and defended by infantry and guns. General Bachelu, whose division led Reille's column, threw away two hours before he finally cleared the passage at Marchienne. Even then, the bridge being narrow, it took four hours for Reille's corps to defile over the river; and d'Erlon's corps in consequence did not even begin to cross until half-past four.

Pajol having failed to carry the bridge of Charleroi by a charge of hussars, waited till eleven o'clock for the arrival of Vandamme's infantry, which, having started late, was still far away; when up came Napoleon himself with a portion of the Young Guard, which, on learning of Vandamme's mishap, he had brought forward by cross-roads. Under the emperor's direction, the barricade was soon broken down; the Prussians retired, and Pajol detaching one regiment—the 1st Hussars—due north towards Gosselies and Quatre-Bras to clear the front of the left column, led his main body north-east upon Fleurus on the track of the retreating Prussians.

Waiting at Charleroi to watch his troops defile over the river, Napoleon received at about two o'clock a message that the Prussians were showing themselves in force in Gosselies, and directed Reille to march his corps in that direction, sending meanwhile the light cavalry of the Guard under Lefebvre-Desnoëttes to support the 1st Hussars. D'Erlon was presently instructed to follow Reille, and Ney, reporting himself to the emperor at three o'clock, was bidden to take command of this, the left wing, proceed to Gosselies and advance along the road to Brussels. At half-past three orders were sent to Gérard to make for the bridge at Châtelet instead of that at Charleroi, as originally ordered; and meanwhile, as Vandamme's and Grouchy's troops debouched from the bridge, they were pushed north-eastward along the road to Gilly.

To deal first with the left wing, Reille's advanced cavalry was checked at Jumet by some of Ziethen's light horse and sharp-shooters, who were covering the retirement of Steinmetz's brigade from Fontaine l'Évêque through Gosselies upon Fleurus. After some delay the mounted troops on both sides came into collision; but there was no decisive result until the French infantry, which had been hurried forward by Reille, came up, drove the sharp-shooters from Gosselies and occupied the village. Steinmetz's main body at this moment was still to west of Gosselies and therefore cut off from the direct road to Fleurus; but with great decision he launched such troops as he had at hand upon the French as they issued from the village, drove them back and, by holding in force the houses at the north end, was able to draw off the bulk of his brigade north-eastward to Heppignies and so to its appointed destination. However, the road to Brussels was now thrown open; and Ney, who had come up in the course of the combat, pushed Lefebvre-Desnoëttes's cavalry northward upon Quatre-Bras and directed Bachelu's infantry to follow him for three miles, as far as Mellet, in support.

Lefebvre-Desnoëttes met with no resistance until he reached Frasnes, about five miles north of Gosselies, where he came upon a battalion and a battery of Prince Bernhard of Saxe-Weimar's Nassau brigade, which lay in and about Quatre-Bras. The village had been prepared for defence; and, as the Nassauers showed a resolute front, Lefebvre sent a party round the eastern flank of his opponents, who thereupon retired to the border of the wood of Bossu, about a mile and a half to the south of Quatre-Bras.

Following them up, Lefebvre found himself stopped abruptly by superior forces at this point; for Prince Bernhard of Saxe-Weimar, anticipating the orders of his divisional commander, Perponcher, had concentrated his brigade at Quatre-Bras and had sent two more battalions and a battery to reinforce his advanced party. Having only cavalry, and those of inferior numbers, under his hand, Lefebvre realised that it was impossible for him to attack. It was now nearly seven o'clock; and, even if he were to summon infantry from Gosselies, they could hardly come up before dark. He therefore fell back for the night to Frasnes, where a battalion of infantry joined him soon after sunset. He then sent in his report to Ney, giving the important information, gleaned from prisoners, that the troops which he had encountered at Frasnes had nothing to do with those that had been engaged at Gosselies. The latter, he explained, had retired eastward upon Fleurus; the former were under Wellington's command; and the bulk of the Netherlandish army lay westward about Mons with headquarters at Braine-le-Comte.[16]

In the centre Pirch II. had occupied a strong position in rear of Gilly, with his front covered by a boggy rivulet; his seven battalions being skilfully disposed to present a great appearance of strength, and his flank towards the Sambre being watched by a regiment of dragoons. Grouchy, who had galloped forward to reconnoitre, would not venture to attack without orders; whereupon Napoleon hurried to the spot and, taking in the situation at a glance, directed him to assail Pirch II.'s front with one of Vandamme's divisions, to turn his left flank with Exelmans's corps of cavalry and to push on to Sombreffe.

This done—the time being about half-past three—the emperor returned to Charleroi to hasten the march of Vandamme's infantry; but, hearing no sound of an engagement, he rode back soon after half-past five to Gilly and ordered Vandamme and Grouchy to attack immediately. Pirch II. thereupon began to retire, and, though some of his battalions were caught and very severely handled by the French cavalry, he made good his retreat with some loss to Fleurus, and was there allowed to rest in peace. Pajol's and Exelmans's troopers then bivouacked to south of Fleurus, covering Vandamme's infantry; and Vandamme and Pajol sent in their reports to the emperor. Vandamme's was to the effect that the Prussians, whom he reckoned at ten to fifteen thousand men, were in full retreat, having left only outposts of cavalry in Fleurus; and Pajol confirmed this by stating that, if Vandamme had given him some infantry, he could have taken Fleurus. Their testimony therefore avouched the fact that the Allies had withdrawn towards the north-east.

On the right, Gérard's corps, having marched upon Charleroi, was delayed rather than hastened by the order that changed its direction to Châtelet, and hence only one of his divisions had crossed the Sambre

---

16. A translation of the full text of this letter is printed by Col. James *Campaign of 1815.*

before dark.

At nightfall therefore the French were thus posted according to Napoleon's distribution into two wings and a reserve. Of the right wing Pajol's and Exelmans's cavalry lay between Lambusart and Campinaire; Vandamme's corps in and to the east of Soleilmont forest; Hulot's division of Gérard's corps at Châtelineau, and the three remaining divisions south of the Sambre at Châtelet. Of the left wing the light cavalry of the Guard was at Frasnes. Reille's corps was banked up in rear of it on the road to Brussels. D'Erlon's corps was at Marchienne, Bachelu's division lying at Mellet, Foy's and Jerome's in and about Gosselies, and Girard's division a little further to the east at Wangenies. Of the Reserve, the Young Guard was at Gilly, the Old Guard between that village and Charleroi, and the whole of Lobau's corps on the south bank of the Sambre.

On the whole, therefore, Napoleon's first day's work had prospered. He had not reached the road which was the line of junction between the inner flanks of the Allies—the road, that is to say, which runs south-eastward from Nivelles to Namur—nor had he thrown more than two-thirds of his army across the Sambre; but he had struck the advanced guards of both of the Allied armies and had found no main body massed behind them. He had met with brave but not very strenuous resistance; he had inflicted substantial loss—some twelve hundred killed, wounded and prisoners—upon Ziethen's corps; and the two Allied armies had retired by divergent routes, the Netherlanders to the north and the Prussians to the east. So far, then, all seemed to promise well for his plan of forcing those two armies apart and beating each of them independently of the other.

On the side of the Allies the fact of the French advance became known to General Ziethen at half-past four in the morning of the 15th, through the sound of Reille's cannon and musketry when he fell upon Steinmetz's brigade at Thuin. Ziethen at once sent information to Blücher and fired the guns which gave the signal of alarm. At a quarter-past eight he despatched a second message reporting that the French had pushed back the Prussian advanced parties and had crossed the Sambre in force, that Napoleon was present in person with his Guard, and that the brigades of Steinmetz and Pirch II. were falling back to Gosselies and Gilly. He added that he had sent this intelligence to Wellington, with a request that the duke should concentrate his army at Nivelles, in accordance with an intimation which General Müffling, Prussian *attaché* at the British headquarters, had given on the previous day.

To the first of these despatches Blücher replied that the IInd, IIIrd and IVth Corps had been ordered to concentrate, and that by evening they would be respectively at Onoz and Mazy, at Namur and at Hannut; and he added injunctions to observe the enemy closely, and to watch the old Roman road and in particular the neighbourhood of Binche. The substance of the second despatch was at once forwarded to Wellington's headquarters by Gneisenau, with the further intelligence that the Prussian headquarters would presently be transferred to Sombreffe, where they would await intelligence of Wellington's intentions. The whole of the Prussian Army would likewise assemble on the morning of the 16th at Sombreffe, where Blücher intended to accept battle.

On Wellington's side of the field the Prince of Orange rode out at five in the morning to St. Symphorien, two miles east of Mons, whence, finding all quiet, he rode to Brussels to dine with Wellington. At noon there reached his head-quarters at Braine-le-Comte a letter from General Behr at Mons, reporting a French attack upon General Steinmetz and a lively fire about Charleroi, and adding that there was no sign of the enemy about Mons. This missive was at once forwarded by General Constant de Rebecque to Brussels, where the Prince of Orange communicated it to Wellington at three o'clock in the afternoon. A little later, further information came into Braine-le-Comte from General Chassé at Haine St. Pierre and General van Merlen at St. Symphorien, confirming the purport of Behr's letter, but containing the additional details that Steinmetz had evacuated Binche and would collect his brigade first at Gosselies.

At two o'clock Constant forwarded this news also to Wellington; and apparently at about the same time he sent orders to Perponcher to assemble his 1st brigade on the paved road near Nivelles, and his 2nd at Quatre-Bras, and to Generals Chassé and Collaert to gather their divisions together, the former at Fayt, the latter behind the Haine. Prince Bernhard of Saxe-Weimar had already placed his brigade in position at Quatre-Bras before receipt of any instruction from Perponcher; but it does not appear that he sent in any report to Brussels of the approach of the French to his front.

The next intelligence, therefore, that Wellington received, so far as can be conjectured, was that despatched by Ziethen from Charleroi at nine in the morning, which arrived between three and four o'clock; the rider having taken six hours to traverse thirty-four miles. An hour or so later Constant's second report came in. Müffling pressed Wellington to say whether he would concentrate his army, and where. The duke answered that until he had further intelligence from Mons—for his latest report from that quarter was of half-past ten in the morning—he could not say, but that he would direct the whole army to be in readiness to march at any moment. This accordingly he did at six o'clock, [17] and at the same time he directed the Fourth Division on his extreme right to close in eastward from Oudenarde to Grammont.

Further, the Prince of Orange was instructed to assemble the 2nd and 3rd Netherlandish divisions at Nivelles, and, if that place should have been attacked in course of the day, to summon thither also the First and Third British Divisions. At seven o'clock Müffling sent the purport of these orders to Gneisenau, adding that the Reserve, or a part of it, would move southward from Brussels when the moon rose. He also gave Wellington's judgment of the situation by the light of the very imperfect intelligence so far supplied to him. The enemy—such was the duke's view—intended either to follow the Sambre downward in order to join other columns which were coming up from the direction of Givet, or to attack in the neighbourhood of Fleurus and, in all probability, in that of Nivelles at the same time. Wellington's object was to be in position to meet this latter onslaught. If it were not delivered, then he would bring the whole of his force to Nivelles on the morrow, ready to support the Prussians, or, if the Prussians should have been already assailed, to fall upon the enemy's flank and rear according to the arrangement already concerted with Blücher.

Some time later, probably near eight o'clock, came in Gneisenau's letter, which had been despatched from Namur soon after noon. Here again the bearer had failed in his duty, for he had taken from seven to eight hours to traverse forty miles. The contents of the letter did little to improve Wellington's knowledge. Gneisenau stated that Ziethen had orders not to retire beyond Fleurus if he could possibly help it; and from this Wellington might infer that the bulk of the enemy's force had turned eastward; but there was not a word to show that this was actually the case. There was not even a hint to indicate that Charleroi was in the enemy's hands. The news of the Prussian concentration at Sombreffe was really no news but simply a confirmation of an existing understanding.

Once again, therefore, Wellington said that he must await intelligence from Mons before deciding upon the rendezvous for his army;

---

17. The date 5 p.m. in *Wellington Desp.* is a mistake or a misprint. See James.

and it was not until ten o'clock that a letter came in from Dörnberg to say that there was nothing on his front. Thereupon Wellington sent out orders for the Reserve to march southward from Brussels to the cross-roads at Mont St. Jean, and for the rest of the army to make a general movement eastward, the cavalry, Second and Fourth Divisions upon Enghien, the First Division upon Braine-le-Comte, and the Third Division upon Nivelles. This done, he went, together with most of his superior officers, to a ball given by the Duchess of Richmond in Brussels, hoping by his presence to discourage sanguine enemies and to hearten desponding friends.

Thus it was that when the hundred and twenty thousand men of Napoleon were bivouacked compactly within the quadrilateral Frasnes, Fleurus, Châtelet, Marchienne, Wellington's army was dispersed practically over the entire extent of its original cantonments, while Blücher's had hardly begun its concentration. It is idle to contend that the Allies were not, in the military sense, surprised; but, masterly though was Napoleon's assembly of his troops, it was very greatly facilitated by the screen of fortresses and forest that lay ready to his hand, and far more than has been hitherto supposed by the fact that, so long as he remained within the boundaries of France, the Allies would not send even a patrol of cavalry to watch his movements.

They could not have ventured to take the offensive and invade France without a declaration of their intentions, whereas it was open to Napoleon to cross the border and create a state of war whenever it might best suit him. "The enemy opened hostilities this morning," are the first words of Gneisenau's letter to Wellington; and, though this had been in a manner expected, yet such temerity as Napoleon's in bearding a force of twice his strength was in itself something of a surprise. Nevertheless, the backwardness of Wellington's concentration was due in great measure to avoidable causes. The Prussians fought their "delaying actions" sturdily and well; but their success shows that, if they had made better preparation for the defence and for the ultimate destruction of the bridges, they could have gained more time for the troops to assemble in their rear.

More blameworthy by far was the omission of the Prussian staff to keep Wellington informed of the course of their proceedings during the day. It appears that Ziethen ceased to consider it his duty to report to the British commander-in-chief immediately after active operations had begun, that is to say, precisely at the moment when it was most necessary that Wellington should be fully apprised of all that was going forward. It was really monstrous that tidings of vital import should have been sent from Fleurus to Brussels by way of Namur, and that a journey of thirty miles should have been lengthened to nearly sixty. The tardiness of the despatch-riders was also disagreeably conspicuous; and Wellington in after years commented with biting humour on the fact that the fattest man in the Prussian Army had been selected to carry to him a message which should have been transmitted with all possible speed. It will be seen that these were not solitary examples of the inefficiency of the Prussian staff.

Quatre Bras

At the Duchess of Richmond's ball Wellington was ostentatiously light of heart; but towards one o'clock on the morning of the 16th when the party had sat down to supper, a third messenger came in from Constant to the Prince of Orange with the news that the French had advanced up to Quatre Bras. Constant added that he had ordered Perponcher to push forward his 1st brigade to the support of Prince Bernhard's, and had warned Chassé and Collaert to be prepared to march with the 3rd Netherlandish Division and the cavalry to the help of Perponcher.

It will be remembered that Wellington's orders of six o'clock had directed Perponcher's and Chassé's divisions to assemble at Nivelles. These orders came to Constant's hand, it seems, immediately after the despatch of his own instructions to Perponcher; but with excellent judgment he took upon himself to disregard them, and to rely upon his own reading of the situation. Wellington with perfect coolness explained the state of affairs to his superior officers, and, after bidding them all withdraw as quietly and speedily as possible to their posts, left the ball at two o'clock and went to bed. He was awakened two or three hours later by General Dörnberg, who had ridden in from Mons, and to whom he gave instructions to hasten at once to Mont St. Jean and order Picton's division forward to Quatre Bras.

Thanks to the foresight of Constant, that important point on the road of communication between the two Allied armies was temporarily secure; and, with the rest of his force at Nivelles, Braine-le-Comte and Enghien, the Duke was prepared to meet attack either on the direct road from Charleroi to Brussels or further to westward between Charleroi and Mons. But towards seven o'clock Wellington decided definitely that Quatre Bras was his true point of concentration, and issued further instructions for a continued eastward movement of the whole army upon that village, Genappe and Nivelles. Though it was still uncertain whether the French advance along the road from Charleroi to Brussels was made in any force, it was clear that, in any case, the Anglo-Netherlandish army must be at hand to support the Prussians if Napoleon's attack should be delivered against them.

The main significance of the reports brought in to Napoleon on the night of the 15th was that the Prussians had retired eastward, and the outposts of Wellington's army towards the north. He judged therefore that his primary object was attained. He had placed his own army between the two Allied hosts, and he was free to fall upon whichever of them he pleased to select. He had already decided that, of the twain, it would be preferable to attack first that of Blücher, whose fiery temperament would prompt him to fly to the succour of Wellington, whereas the British general, whom he judged to be slow and circumspect, would be less eager to march to the support of his Prussian colleague. It is characteristic of Napoleon that it never occurred to him that two commanders might act with unselfish loyalty towards each other. Good faith, upon principle and not for personal advantage, was a matter that lay beyond his horizon: he had always lied to his generals in Spain and they had always lied to him. [1]

Had he been concerned with Gneisenau instead of with Blücher, his diagnosis of character would have been less incorrect; for Gneisenau was equally ignorant of the meaning of good faith, so much so, indeed, that the mere study of his character has infected one of his biographers with the same failing. However, having made this false assumption, Napoleon built his plan of campaign upon it. At four o'clock in the morning he sent an officer to Frasnes to learn how affairs stood in that quarter; and an hour later Soult despatched orders to Ney to ascertain the exact position of Reille's and d'Erlon's corps.

Before eight o'clock the emperor formulated his plan of operations for the day. Grouchy and the right wing were to march northeastward upon Sombreffe and Gembloux, and to fall upon any Prussian corps that might be found in either position. Gérard's corps might be called in, if needed, for the attack on Sombreffe; but the emperor did not expect to be opposed by more than forty thousand Prussians.

1. On the evening of this same 15th of June he had issued a bulletin claiming in one passage that the day's operations had cost the Prussians 2600 men, of which 1000 prisoners: and in another that 400 to 500 men had been sabred and 1750 captured—all at a cost to the French of 10 killed and 80 wounded. *Carres, de Napoléon*, 22056.

He himself would reach Fleurus between ten and eleven o'clock, leave the whole of his Guard there, and push on alone to Sombreffe. Having ascertained that Sombreffe and Gembloux were clear of the enemy, he would lead his reserve to join the left wing at Quatre Bras, from whence both united would make a night march northward and by seven o'clock in the morning of the 17th should have reached Brussels. He impressed upon Ney the importance of occupying Brussels, which, as he reckoned, might produce great results; for so prompt and sudden a march would isolate the British from Mons and Ostend.

These orders show that on the morning of the 16th Napoleon's ideas of the whereabouts of his enemy were of the vaguest. He evidently did not expect to find Blücher in force either at Sombreffe or at Gembloux, and, supposing that his expectations proved to be correct, he considered it safe to infer that the Prussians had withdrawn to a secure distance eastward, and that he could devote his principal attention to Wellington. Equally he expected to find the British in retreat. In the supplementary orders sent by Soult to Ney, it was enjoined upon the latter to occupy Quatre Bras with two corps of infantry and one of cavalry, push on a division of infantry and some cavalry to Genappe, and send out reconnaissances towards Brussels and Nivelles, upon which latter point the Anglo-Netherlanders would probably have retreated. In other words, he looked that the bare terror of his advance between them should have caused both of their armies to retreat, each towards its own base, in opposite directions, which was the very thing that Blücher and Wellington had agreed not to do.

Against this inference, however, must be set the remarkable allusion to Mons and Ostend in the letter to Ney; for, if the British were retiring to the west, it is very clear that a rapid advance from Quatre Bras to Brussels would isolate them from neither the one place nor the other. Indeed, if Wellington, upon the news of Ney's rapid advance, should face about and march eastward, he would fall full upon the Emperor's flank. On the other hand, if we assume that the advance to Brussels was deliberately conceived with the idea of cutting Wellington's communications to westward, then obviously Napoleon expected the Anglo-Netherlandish Army to be at Brussels or to east of it. In that case Wellington's purpose was not to be mistaken. He intended to sacrifice his line of operations with Ostend rather than his contact with the Prussian Army; and, as we have seen, the duke had promised Gneisenau that he would take this course in the event of a retreat.

Had some inkling of this promise and of Wellington's extreme anxiety to preserve Brussels and Ghent reached the emperor's ears? If it had, and if he really believed that the duke had retired north and eastward, then evidently his plan of falling upon the Allied armies in detail and beating them separately was already wrecked. Meanwhile, he was for the present too prudent to take anything unverified for granted. He told Ney plainly that his final decision could not be made until the afternoon or evening, after he had explored the ground as far as Gembloux; and he bade the marshal post a division at Marbais, as a central point between Quatre Bras, Sombreffe and Gembloux, so that he could summon it to the support of the right wing in case of need.

Moreover, the division at Marbais was instructed to throw out reconnaissances in every direction, particularly towards Gembloux and even towards Wavre, the latter place being nearly fourteen miles due north of Sombreffe. This indicates that the emperor kept in view the possibility that the two Allied armies might make a convergent retreat towards the north. In fact, he was utterly in the dark as to the actual positions and intentions of his enemies; and his conjectures were founded upon the false hypothesis that the defeat which he had inflicted upon the Prussians was so serious as to make retreat the only possible course for both armies.

On the evening of the 15th the Prussian Army was still for the most part far from its point of concentration, the IInd Corps being between Mazy and Onoz, and the Vth near Namur; but orders had been sent to hasten them forward, and some of them were on march during the night. The IVth corps was hopelessly out of reach. Gneisenau had sent Bülow only a polite request, instead of a positive order, to move to Hannut on the 15th; and the latter general, ignorant that hostilities had begun, ignorant that a general concentration of the army was in progress, and thinking that, if it were, it would take place at Hannut, made no speed to arrive at the place betimes, and was still far east of it when night fell.

Fresh orders were despatched by Blücher to Hannut late in the forenoon of the 15th, bidding Bülow hasten to Gembloux at the earliest possible hour on the 16th; but, as Bülow was not at Hannut, the letter did not reach him until hard upon midnight, when he returned the inevitable answer, that it was physically impossible for his corps to reach Gembloux at the appointed time. At about the same hour Gneisenau recalled Ziethen's corps from Fleurus to Sombreffe, and by eight o'clock in the morning of the 16th it was assembled in position between St. Amand and Ligny; the IInd and IIIrd Corps being still far in rear.

By that time it is to be presumed that Müffling's last letter from Brussels had come to Blücher's hand; and at half-past ten there reached him a note from a Prussian *aide-de-camp,* who had been sent at five o'clock in the morning to Quatre Bras, reporting that the French were still at Frasnes and that their patrols had interrupted communication between the two armies for a time during the night, but that the Prince of Orange expected the whole of the Netherlandish army and most of the British to be concentrated near Nivelles by ten o'clock. At about eleven o'clock Pirch I.'s corps came up and was placed provisionally between the Roman road and Sombreffe; and an hour later Thielmann's corps likewise presented itself and was arrayed on the left of Pirch's from Sombreffe to Tongrinne. The total force thus assembled numbered about eighty-two thousand men with two hundred and twenty-four guns.

The Prince of Orange, meanwhile, had left Brussels in haste and reached his headquarters at Braine-le-Comte at half-past three. After a few words with Constant he confirmed all the orders given by the chief of his staff, who then rode off to Quatre Bras. Acting with a strength of initiative not less admirable than Constant's own, Perponcher had kept Prince Bernhard's brigade in its former station and had brought down half of his 2nd brigade, Bijlandt's, to support it. On his way Constant sent forward Bijlandt's two remaining battalions and artillery from Nivelles to join their division, and on reaching Quatre Bras found Perponcher already engaged in making his dispositions and in driving back the French advanced posts. At six o'clock the Prince of Orange arrived and, by Perponcher's advice, extended his front to give a greater appearance of strength. He sent Constant to Nivelles to look to the disposition of Chassé's division and of Alten's which, once again through the initiative of Constant, had been bidden to continue its march from Soignies to Nivelles.

He also despatched orders to the Guards to continue their march from Braine-le-Comte to the same place—orders which miscarried, for Cooke did not receive them until he reached Nivelles in the afternoon, having proceeded thither by his own motion. In the course of these proceedings Blücher's *aide-de-camp* arrived and was sent back with the answer which has already been quoted; and at seven o'clock the prince reported his proceedings to Wellington, adding that the French were at Frasnes, with both infantry and cavalry, but not as yet in force. There was in fact nothing so far to show that the French advance upon the road to Brussels might not after all be a feint, disguising a turning movement further to the west.

So the morning of the 16th wore on. At nine o'clock the Allies had still only six thousand five hundred men and eight guns at Quatre Bras; and shortly after that hour Wellington arrived. From some stragglers of Steinmetz's brigade he at length learned some details of what had happened on the previous day, how the French had crossed the Sambre at Charleroi and Marchienne, had driven Ziethen back after sharp encounters at Fleurus and Gosselies, and had penetrated by patrols as far as the road between Sombreffe and Quatre Bras. He appeared surprised and indeed incredulous, as well he might, for not the slightest report of these things had been sent to him from any Prussian source; but he congratulated the Prince of Orange and Perponcher upon their courage in acting upon their own judgment, and approved their dispositions in every particular.

Riding forward to reconnoitre for himself, he found that he could see nothing owing to woods and folds of ground, and, as the Prince of Orange had no cavalry with him, the duke was obliged to be content with conjecture. At half-past ten, having at last ascertained the whereabouts of Blücher, he wrote him a letter to the effect that the Prince of Orange's corps was at Quatre Bras and Nivelles, that the Reserve and the British cavalry were on march and would reach Genappe and Nivelles at noon, that Hill was at Braine-le-Comte, that he himself could perceive no great force of the enemy before him, and that he awaited news from the Prussian headquarters and the arrival of his troops before deciding upon the day's operations. This intelligence, supplied to Wellington by his staff, was very inaccurate, as the subsequent narrative will prove; but the duke furnished it in good faith and based his own actions upon the assumed truth of it. The insinuations of German writers, that he wrote this letter with the deliberate purpose of deceiving Blücher and making him fight a battle to cover the concentration of the Anglo-Netherlandish army, deserve nothing more than contempt. [2]

---

2. It is a pity that General Pollio (French translation) should write: "*Sortons du champ des suppositions Wellington était peut-être plus diplomate que général, il faisait partie du cabinet anglais bien qu'éloigné de Londres, il occupait une position très élevée, supérieure à celle de Blücher, et il s'attribuait en outre une telle supériorité dans son orgueil brittannique qu'il a probablement cru agir avec Blücher comme il avait agi dans la Péninsule avec ses alliés portugais et espagnols.*" It is well when quitting the domain of conjecture at least not to exchange it for that of fiction, not to say falsehood. Wellington was certainly an able diplomatist, but he did not base his diplomacy upon deceit, as General Pollio quite gratuitously assumes. He was not a member of the British Cabinet, to which he seldom wrote more acrimonious letters than during this (continued next page),

Shortly afterwards the duke rode on with Müffling to Ligny to see Blücher. He met the old field-marshal near Brye on the right of the chosen battlefield, where the troops were already forming for the combat; and he observed with astonishment that they were so arrayed on the forward slope of the hill that no cannon-shot could help striking the supports and reserves, even if it should miss the fighting line. He protested mildly. "Every man knows his own troops best," he hinted; "but if my troops were so disposed I should expect them to be beaten."

Such criticism, however gently advanced, was not likely to commend itself to a theorist such as Gneisenau, who, besides, was more concerned with the help that Wellington might be able to afford him than with his own dispositions. The duke, who was still inclined to think that the French were only making a demonstration before Frasnes, had, during the ride to Ligny, declared to Müffling his willingness to bring his whole force, if possible, to the assistance of the Prussians; and, though no record of his conversation with Blücher is preserved, there can be no doubt that he repeated to the field-marshal the substance of the words which he had already used to the *attaché*. From the mill of Bussy, which commanded a great extent of ground, the French columns could be seen advancing to the attack; and Gneisenau, thinking that practically the whole French Army was before him, urged the duke to bring as large a force as possible to Brye to act as a reserve to the Prussian Army. Wellington, supported by Müffling, was inclined rather to overthrow the French force before him at Quatre Bras and march on Gosselies, that is to say upon the rear of the main French Army. The discussion was closed by Wellington, who said, "Well, I will come, if I am not attacked myself"; and therewith he started to ride back to Quatre Bras. It was then apparently between half-past one and two o'clock.

Let us return now to the French side. Ney received in succession Napoleon's own order and Soult's, which was to the same effect, somewhere about eleven o'clock. He answered at that hour that he

---

short campaign. Finally, any one conversant with the history of the Peninsular war (which no foreigner is, and General Pollio very manifestly is not) would know that, even if it were true that Wellington endeavoured to save himself by deceiving Blücher, no parallel case could be adduced from his relations with the Spaniards and Portuguese. General Pollio evidently is not even aware that the Portuguese troops were commanded by a British General, paid by the British Treasury, and mingled in every division with British troops—a pretty critic to pronounce judgment on Wellington whether as general, diplomatist or man.

was making his dispositions accordingly, that there appeared to be only three thousand infantry and a very few cavalry in his front, and that, in his opinion, there would be little obstacle in the way of the Emperor's dispositions for the march on Brussels.

Meanwhile Napoleon, having given Grouchy his orders and summoned Gérard to bring the whole of his corps across the Sambre and lead it straight upon Sombreffe, prepared to ride to Fleurus. Just before he started he received, apparently some time before ten o'clock, a message from the left wing, stating that the enemy was showing considerable strength at Quatre Bras; whereupon he forwarded to Ney through Soult the following order, which was little more than a confirmation of those already despatched.

> Assemble Reille's and d'Erlon's corps, and Kellermann's, which will march to join you at once. With these you should be able to defeat and destroy any force of the enemy that might present themselves. Blücher was at Namur yesterday, and is not likely to have sent troops to Quatre Bras, so you will have none but those that come from Brussels to deal with.

Here again we meet with the same confusion of thought as appears in Napoleon's first order already quoted. What did he mean by "the force coming from Brussels?" Why should no hostile force come up from the west? Or, if the British at large were retiring westward, why should they march southward from Brussels at all, when they could join the general retreat by moving by the great road to Ninove? On the other hand, if a French advance upon Brussels was to cut the British of from the base at Ostend, obviously the bulk of the British force must be to east or north-east of Brussels, in which case their movement southward from the capital might be very formidable.

But still more remarkable is the fact that the purport of the message delivered to Napoleon as to the strength of the Allies at Quatre Bras must have been made known to Ney before he wrote his answer to the emperor's first orders, and that, having once declared the force at that village to be trifling, he was at no pains to contradict it. The French commanders one and all seem to have based their plans upon hypotheses which they took not the slightest pains to verify by reconnaissance.

At about eleven o'clock Napoleon reached Fleurus and, ascending to the summit of a mill, surveyed Blücher's position at Ligny. He reckoned correctly that he had only one corps before him, though there were signs already of the approach of others, and resolved to attack at once, but was annoyed to find that Gérard's corps had not come up. Soult had sent off his orders to Gérard between seven and eight o'clock, but they seem to have taken two hours to travel four miles, for they did not come to hand until half-past nine, or at any rate Gérard did not set his troops in motion until that hour. It was then necessary for them to defile across the narrow bridge at Châtelet, and thus it was half-past one before they reached the field of action.

At two o'clock the emperor sent through Soult a fourth message to Ney, which conditionally cancelled the previous instructions respecting the march to Brussels. Its purport was that the Prussians had assembled a corps between Sombreffe and Brye, which would be attacked by Grouchy with the 3rd and 4th Corps at half-past two. Ney was therefore required to drive back with vigour whatever hostile troops might be in front of him, and, having done so, to fall back towards the right wing so as to envelop the Prussians aforesaid. If, on the other hand, the Emperor should have already defeated them, he would manoeuvre in Ney's direction to hasten the accomplishment of the operations prescribed to the Marshal.

At three o'clock Napoleon's dispositions were complete and he ordered the attack to begin. He had at his disposal the 3rd and 4th Corps (Vandamme's and Gérard's), Girard's division of Reille's corps, Lobau's corps, which was ordered forward from Charleroi just as the battle began, also Pajol's, Exelmans's and Milhaud's corps of cavalry, in all seventy-six thousand men, or deducting Lobau's corps, which was not actually on the spot, sixty-five thousand men. By this time Napoleon was alive to the fact that he had before him not a corps but an army; but he was elated rather than depressed by the fact, for he asked nothing better than to have done with Blücher at a stroke. "The issue of this war may be decided in three hours," he said. "If Ney executes my orders properly, not a gun of this army will escape"; and therewith he despatched to Ney a fifth set of instructions.

We are heavily engaged with the Prussians (such was its purport), manoeuvre at once so as to envelope their right and fall with clenched fists upon their rear. If you act with vigour this army of theirs is lost. The fate of France is in your hands. Lose not a moment in marching on the heights of St. Amand and Brye, to share in what may be a decisive victory.

These instructions completely ignored the possibility that Ney might have an enemy in front of him; and, just at the moment, as it happened, a letter reached the Emperor from Lobau, telling him that Ney was confronted with twenty thousand men at Quatre Bras. The news did not disconcert Napoleon. If Ney could not spare his whole army, he must hold the enemy before him in check with Reille's corps only, and send d'Erlon's to make the turning movement upon Blücher's right. Napoleon accordingly sent an order to this effect to Ney.

The Battle of Ligny forms no part of the history of the British Army, and only the briefest summary of its course can be given here. Napoleon opened the fight by a vigorous attack upon Blücher's right and centre, which was met by as strenuous a defence, and by counter-attacks which were resisted by the French with a stubbornness equal to that of the Prussians themselves. After more than two hours of a bitter struggle no ground had been gained by either party; and, since Lobau's corps was now approaching, Napoleon resolved to launch the Guard to a supreme attack against the Prussian centre; hoping to cleave the army in twain, surround the right wing with the help of d'Erlon, and drive the left wing eastward upon Namur.

The dispositions had been made and the attack was about to begin when the emperor was informed that a strong hostile column was bearing down upon his left flank, and in fact that the French troops in that quarter were falling back in disorder, or, in plain words, running away. Perforce he suspended the assault of his Guard and sent half of them to strengthen the threatened flank. Blücher seized the moment to aim a great counter-stroke at the French left. He was, however, repulsed, and presently the emperor learned that the supposed hostile column was d'Erlon's corps. So intense seems to have been his relief at this welcome tidings that he forgot everything else in the renewal of his attack upon the Prussian centre; while d'Erlon, who had just received a pressing order from Ney to return to Quatre Bras, counter-marched and left the field of Ligny behind him.

By about seven o'clock all was ready; and after a heavy cannonade the Guard were let loose to the assault. Blücher, having already used up his reserves on his right, had little infantry with which to meet them. The gallant old warrior therefore led his reserve cavalry in person to the charge, but his troops could make no impression upon the Guard, and were repulsed with great loss. His horse was shot under him, and while on the ground he was ridden over and trampled on, only escaping at last on a sergeant's horse, bruised, shaken, and hardly conscious. The whole of the Prussian centre broke up in disorder, and

Marbais

Pon

JUNGAS

Aux trois Burettes

TIPPELSKIRCHEN

P

I R C H

ROMAN ROAD

KRAFFT BRAUSE

Bry

PIRCH

LANCAN

Wagnele

NA

Mill of Bussy

St Amand
La Haye

Hameau
de St Amand

N

From Mellet

VANDAMM

DOMONT

GERARD

Tombe
de Ligny

St Amand

VICHERY

Brook

Fleurus

Wagnée

orieux · Vieille Manon · Humrée · BORCKE · STOLNAGEL · Botey

Sombuef · Le Point du Jour · JAGER · ELEMANN · Tongrines · KAMPFEN · MORE

GNY · Ligny · Tongrenelles · Boignee · Balatre · Ligny Ry

GROUCHY · old road to Namur · Velaine sur les Pierres · mérée

BATTLE OF LIGNY
at ½ past 2 o'clock p.m.
SCALE
0   ¼   ½   ¾   1 Mile

———— Prussians
———— French

BATTLE OF LIGNY
at ½ past 8 o'clock p.m

SCALE

Prussians
French

the battle was lost. Sixty-five thousand French had beaten eighty-three thousand Prussians, through the fault, not of the Prussian rank and file, but of Gneisenau and his colleagues of the staff, who had chosen a very defective position in the first place and defended it very unskilfully in the second. With a superiority of nearly four to three they should certainly have given a better account of Napoleon; and it is childish to contend, as German writers have with unblushing effrontery contended, that Blücher would not have accepted battle had he not counted upon help from Wellington. Blücher was firmly resolved to fight in any circumstances; [3] and, if his tactical skill had been equal to his courage and constancy, the result would amply have justified his determination.

On the French left wing Ney, apparently confident that he would meet with little resistance at Quatre Bras, made no preparations for an advance before receiving the emperor's commands. Nor were these, as we have seen, at the outset of a nature to demand particular activity or haste, since they gave him to understand that no serious work would be expected of him before nightfall. He issued therefore no orders for the march of his infantry upon the road to Brussels until eleven o'clock, which signified that Reille's divisions were not fairly in movement before noon, and that the head of the column did not reach Frasnes until half-past one. At this spot there were already Bachelu's division, about five thousand men, Pire's and Lefebvre-Desnoëttes's light cavalry, rather under four thousand men, and twenty-six guns.

The hamlet of Quatre Bras lies at the intersection of the roads that lead from Brussels to Charleroi and from Nivelles to Namur, at a point about two and a half miles due north of Frasnes. On an elevation, slightly higher than the undulating ground on every side, stood a very large farmhouse and buildings, with a few labourers' cottages, all clustered about the actual cross-roads.

To westward of the cross the Namur road passes through a deep cutting to an embankment, and to eastward from an embankment to a cutting, forming in either case a natural line of defence. From the farm the ground slopes gently southward along the Brussels road to a tiny rivulet which, rising about five hundred yards west of the road, passed under it, and was dammed up about a thousand yards farther east into a wedge-shaped pond, called the Materne Pond, broadening at its eastern end, and measuring about four hundred yards from east to west.

---

3. See James.

64

At the foot of the slope which rises southward from this rivulet, and just on the eastern side of the Brussels road, stood another farm, that of Gemioncourt; and from the rivulet itself, which likewise bears the name of Gemioncourt, the ground ascends gently for some six hundred yards and ripples away southward towards Frasnes, throwing out, however, within eleven hundred yards of Gemioncourt, a well-marked spur to the east, which is defined along its southern flank by a second small rivulet, whose course is parallel to that of Gemioncourt. Near the eastern extremity of this spur and about three-quarters of a mile east of the Brussels road stands another group of farm buildings known as Pireaumont farm. West of the road and nearly a mile south-west of Gemioncourt farm, the farm of Grand Pierrepont marks the source of another rivulet, that of Odomont, which flows through a depression in a south-westerly direction, passing a second farm, Petit Pierrepont, some eight hundred yards on its downward course.

The other main features of the ground were two woods of considerable extent, of which the first, Hutte Wood, extended from a point a little south of Pireaumont for some two thousand yards southward, with a breadth of rather less than a mile east and west. The other wood, that of Bossu, extended west of the Brussels road, practically from Quatre Bras farm to within six hundred yards of Grand Pierrepont, gradually widening out from a breadth of about five hundred yards by Quatre Bras to sixteen hundred yards abreast of Gemioncourt, and then running out into a narrow tongue from the south-western corner towards Pierrepont. This Bossu Wood was of very thick coppice with high but scanty standards, and was traversed by broad rides convenient for the passage of troops.

North of the Namur road yet another smaller wood—Bois des Cerises or Cherry Wood—stretched from the road itself opposite to the Materne Pond almost to the village of Sart-Dame-Avelines. Round the buildings there were orchards and gardens; on the borders of the stream were little thickets and rows of trees; and the open country was covered with tall crops of corn. Altogether the position was blind, and, in the hands of a capable commander, well susceptible of defence; though the Hutte Wood effectively screened the movements of an enemy coming up from the south on the eastern side of the Brussels road.

Guided by the advice of Perponcher, the Prince of Orange extended one battalion in skirmishing order along the spur between the rivulets of Gemioncourt and Pireaumont to the Brussels road,

BATTLE OF
QUATRE BRAS
at 3 o'clock, p.m.

Scale of ½   ½   ½ mile

▭▭▭ ••••• •••• English.
▭▭▭ •••••• •••• French.

From Nivelles

BOSSU

FRENCH

BRUNSWICK

Gémioncourt

JÉROME

Wood

Wood
of
Pierrepont

PIRÉ

Pierrepont

Pierrepont

BATTLE OF
QUATRE BRAS
at 9 o'clock, p.m.

Scale of ⅛ ¼ ½ mile

▣ ▤▦ ↦↦↦ ••• English.
▢ ▥▥ ••••• ••• French.

from Nivelles

D'AUBRÉME

Bossu

Wood

Wood
of

Gemioncourt

Pierrepont

ROUSSEL

p g r

p f r

J. ROME

Pierrepont

QUATRE BRAS

MERLE

BASSE CENSE

Haute Cense

Sart-Dames-
-Avelines

SWICK

KEMPT

FOX

M'Herald

Piermont

Thyle

and thence south-westward along the Odomont rivulet; the farms of Pireaumont and Petit Pierrepont forming the two extremities of the line to left and right, with one battery upon the road in the centre. Next in rear of them four battalions were stationed near the southern border of Bossu Wood, with two more battalions, also in the wood, in support. Another battery was posted at the south-eastern angle of the wood, and between it and Gemioncourt farm, which was strongly occupied; and three more battalions were echeloned along the road from Quatre Bras farm to Gemioncourt.

In all, at two o'clock the prince had at his disposal about seven thousand men with sixteen guns; and at three o'clock the arrival of another battalion, which had been released from Nivelles by the coming of Chassé's and Alten's divisions to that place, increased his number to nearly eight thousand. To hold a good two miles front with so weak a detachment could not but be hazardous; but it was imperative for the moment to make a show of strength; and every credit must be given to Perponcher for the bold face with which he confronted a critical situation.

At about two o'clock the head of Bachelu's division—Husson's brigade—under the personal direction of Reille, debouched on to the plateau at the north-western corner of Hutte Wood. Ney, with Piré's light cavalry of the line and Lefebvre-Desnoëttes's of the Guard, was already on the ground, and had ridden forward with a single *aide-de-camp* to reconnoitre. Unable to see many troops, he concluded that the position was weakly held, and was for assailing Bossu Wood without delay. Reille, however, who had observed the scarlet uniforms of British officers, remembered Wellington's custom of hiding his men, and pleaded that more battalions should be brought up before opening the attack. There was therefore a pause, whilst Bachelu's second brigade and Foy's division came forward to the plateau, when four columns were formed and directed upon the spur between Pireaumont and the Brussels road. On the extreme right or east were Piré's division of cavalry, next to the left of it were the two brigades of Bachelu's division, Campy's on the right and Husson's on the left; and the left column of all was made up of Jamin's brigade of Foy's division. Gauthier's brigade, together with the cavalry of Lefebvre-Desnoëttes and Guiton's *cuirassiers* were held in reserve on the road.

The rest of Kellermann's cavalry corps, to which Guiton's brigade belonged, had been stationed by Ney at Liberchies, about two miles south-west of Frasnes. Jerome's division of infantry was on the march from Gosselies, and d'Erlon's corps was following in rear of it. Altogether Ney could reckon that he had thirty-five thousand infantry, seven thousand cavalry, and ninety-two guns under his hand or within easy call, of which he had detached for his first attack about six thousand infantry, two thousand cavalry, and six guns.

Before the advance of numbers so overwhelming the Netherlandish skirmishers fell back towards Gemioncourt, where Perponcher installed them in and about the buildings; and the Prince of Orange withdrew the two batteries from their advanced positions to a knoll a short distance south of Quatre Bras from which they could rake the Brussels road. Foy then changed the direction of his column to the left, and drove the Netherlanders from Gemioncourt. These retreated hastily up the road, but were unlucky enough to be charged and utterly dispersed by Piré, who, finding his way obstructed by boggy ground, had returned to the highway.

Meanwhile the head of Jerome's column came up, releasing Gauthier's brigade and enabling Ney to press the Netherlanders back from Pierrepont into Bossu Wood. There the French could advance but slowly, for the undergrowth was exceedingly thick, and the Netherlanders offered some resistance. Nevertheless the enemy mastered the borders of the wood and pressed their opponents surely and steadily backward. Let Netherlandish writers say what they will, the initial efforts of their comrades do not appear to have been very strenuous on this day. The advanced posts were not held with the tenacity which the occasion demanded, and the troops did not respond as they ought to the leadership of the gallant young prince and the brave and skilful general who were at their head.

They were now, however, in great measure to redeem their character. Wellington had returned from Ligny; and soon after two o'clock the leading battalions of Picton's division came into sight, [4] Kempt's brigade leading, and the Ninety-fifth, apparently, at the head of the column. Van Merlen's brigade of Netherlandish cavalry arrived at almost the same moment, and the legion of the Duke of Brunswick was following close in the rear of Picton. In the desperate situation of the moment Wellington saw no salvation but in a counter-attack.[5]

He therefore directed the Riflemen to move at once upon Pireau-

---

4. Accounts vary as to the time when Picton's division came up. The head of the column must have come in about 2 p.m.

5. The true significance of this counter-attack is missed, as it seems to me, by all writers except Müffling. Wellington, *Supp. Desp.* 10.

mont and to endeavour to regain it, but at all events to secure Cherry Wood so as to ensure the safety of the Namur road and so of communication with the Prussian Army. At the same time he ordered the Netherlanders to recover Gemioncourt and sent the Twenty-Eighth down to help to hold the buildings. The remainder of Picton's division was diverted round the east side of Quatre Bras, with instructions to align itself along the Namur road, the Ninety-Second forming the right of the line with its right resting on the buildings, and then in succession upon its left, the Forty-second, Forty-Fourth, Royal Scots, Thirty-Second and Seventy-Ninth, [6] with Rogers's battery of artillery on the right and Rettberg's on the left of the array. Best's Hanoverian brigade [7] was ordered to stand in second line behind the British battalions. On the right Prince Bernhard, likewise, was bidden to make a counter-attack and to clear Bossu Wood of the enemy.

These dispositions required some time for their execution, for it was long before the last of the regiments arrived; and meanwhile the Riflemen, before they were halfway to Pireaumont, saw the enemy throw so powerful a force into the farm as to make attack hopeless. Another body of French was pushing on towards Cherry Wood, but here the Riflemen anticipated them, and, throwing their reserve into the wood, lined the road with their skirmishers and engaged the enemy hotly. Gradually the green-jackets extended their line down the road to the hamlet of Thyle, where two companies ensconced themselves in the houses and for the present secured their left flank.

In the centre the Dutch Militia recovered Gemioncourt, and deploying in front of the farm beat off an attack of the French cavalry; but, finding themselves outflanked by the advance of Foy on their right, they were obliged to evacuate the buildings once more. The British Twenty-Eighth, seeing that it had arrived too late, thereupon counter-marched and returned to their division. Prince Bernhard, on his side, took the offensive with great spirit in Bossu Wood, drove the French with the bayonet from a part that they had taken, and, with the help of a fresh battalion sent to him by the Prince of Orange, made shift to maintain the advantage that he had won.

---

6. This order is conjectural. It is, however, certain that the 92nd was on the extreme right and the 79th on the extreme left, also (*Waterloo Letters*, by H.T. Siborne is also published by Leonaur) that the 42nd was on the right of the 44th instead of on the left, as it should have been.

7. This brigade belonged to the Reserve and not to Picton's division at all; but by some mistake had been sent forward with it.

Wellington's counter-stroke had at least gained time for Picton to set his division in order, and for part of the Duke of Brunswick's legion to reach the scene of action; though it had failed to recover the important posts on his centre and left. The possession of Gemioncourt and of the skirts of Bossu Wood enabled Ney to bring forward his whole army without further interruption; and, as he appears to have received at about this time Soult's letter bidding him drive his enemy back and then swing round to attack the Prussians at Brye, he launched his attack along the whole line in earnest. Sixteen guns were massed to east of the Brussels road, and twenty-six between Pireaumont and Gemioncourt.

On his right Bachelu advanced from Pireaumont against the troops on the Namur road; in his centre Foy led his division in two columns along the Brussels road and to the east of it upon Quatre Bras; and on the left Jerome threw Soye's brigade into Bossu Wood and led Bauduin's brigade parallel with Foy's division on the western side of the road. A heavy cannonade heralded the onslaught, and it should seem that Bachelu's division was the first to come to close action, for his sharpshooters were already working deadly mischief among the British gunners before more than the leading section of Rogers's battery had come into action.

The bulk of Picton's division was hidden among the dense crops of rye which covered the fields, and the skirmishers of both sides were hotly engaged, when Wellington suddenly ordered Kempt's brigade to rise and advance. Whether dismayed by the unexpected apparition, or shaken by the British volley, Bachelu's leading regiment, the 2nd Light, broke and fled without awaiting the charge, [8] and the whole division, turning tail, rushed down the hill to the Gemioncourt rivulet and would not be rallied even on the plateau beyond it.

Most of the British battalions pursued no farther than to a hedge at a short distance from the Namur road; but the Forty-Second and Forty-Fourth advanced to within a short distance of Gemioncourt, and the Seventy-Ninth, which by Wellington's order had begun the offensive movement before the rest of the battalions, pressed the chase to the rivulet and even beyond it. Foy, however, observing the rout of Bachelu, had withdrawn the 100th regiment from Jamin's brigade, and, after bidding that officer continue his advance to Quatre Bras,

---

8. This is the account given by Foy, *Girod de l'Ain*. He says that four British battalions charged; but the 95th was still detached from Kempt's brigade, so that there can have been only three.

had betaken himself with the 100th to the plateau south of Gemion-court. It was he who arrested the career of the three battalions, though the Seventy-Ninth, taking shelter behind a fence, fired volleys at the 100th until its ammunition was exhausted.

Not for some time did the Camerons retire, when, on receiving orders to fall back, they stole warily from fence to fence and, covered by the Thirty-Second, regained without serious loss their original position. From a few of the most headlong of the Seventy-Ninth, whom he made prisoners, Foy learned that eight British brigades had just come in from Enghien and Brussels, and that others besides Nether-landers were on march to Quatre Bras. This intelligence he no doubt transmitted to Ney.

On the French left the progress of Soye in Bossu Wood was immediate; raw troops, such as the Netherlanders, having little chance in forest-fighting against veterans; and Wellington, in order to guard their left flank and give them confidence, sent two Brunswick battalions down the road to a point midway between Quatre Bras and Gemioncourt, stationing the Brunswick cavalry immediately behind them. Lastly, he posted two more battalions in the corner of the wood adjoining Quatre Bras with orders to fight to the last extremity.

The foremost of these troops soon suffered heavily from the fire of a French battery on the road above Gemioncourt; and four British guns, which the Duke of Brunswick had borrowed from Wellington and unlimbered by his infantry, were quickly silenced. Shortly afterwards the columns of Jamin, Gauthier and Bauduin approached on both sides of the road, and both Brunswickers and Netherlanders gradually gave way before them. The Duke of Brunswick, taking command of his squadron of lancers, charged the advancing French to cover the retreat of his infantry and hussars, but was beaten back with heavy loss. The lancers fled to the rear of Quatre Bras, whither the hussars also retired in more orderly fashion. One of Brunswick's regiments of infantry, under his personal command, struck eastward from the Brussels road towards Picton's division, but the other, harried by the pursuing French skirmishers and by the round-shot of the French batteries, broke and fled in all directions.

The Duke of Brunswick, hurrying back, tried to rally them under cover of a house and garden called the Bergerie, upon the road about three hundred yards south of Quatre Bras, but fell mortally wounded by a bullet through the body. Now Piré's cavalry, two regiments of *chasseurs* leading and two regiments of lancers in rear, came galloping up the road to complete their success; and the Brunswick Hussars were formed again to meet them, together, it appears, with Van Merlen's cavalry, which had been hastily ordered to the front by the Prince of Orange. Both were overthrown and put to flight without difficulty by the *chasseurs* and they streamed away, some straight up the Brussels road to Quatre Bras, some eastward towards the Namur road. The *chasseurs*, close at the heels of the former, flew up the highway after them, while the lancers, wheeling sharply to their right, took up the chase of those that had turned east; and pursuers and pursued in a mixed body crowded into the angle between the two roads.

The Ninety-Second, which was the last of Picton's battalions to come up, had not long taken up their position, under Wellington's own eye, immediately on the east side of Quatre Bras; the men lying down in the ditch on the south side of the Namur road to gain shelter from the fire of the French batteries in their front. As the *chasseurs* approached them the duke, who was watching the fight a short distance in front of the Highlanders, was obliged to turn and gallop for his life; and, crying to the men to lie still, he put his horse at the ditch, leaped over them, and took his place in rear of the regiment.

As the leading files of the *chasseurs* whirled up the Brussels road, the right-hand company of the Ninety-Second wheeled round parallel to it and poured a destructive fire upon their right flank, while the Brunswickers in the north-eastern angle of Bossu Wood simultaneously rained bullets upon their left flank. This cross-fire fairly cut the column of the *chasseurs* in twain. The rearmost rallied and retired in good order, but the foremost pressed on into the village and beyond it, cutting down stragglers and fugitives; when, finding themselves unable to retreat by the way of their advance, they tried to find egress through the buildings or along the Namur road in rear of the Highlanders, and were shot down to a man. At this point, therefore, the onset of the cavalry was checked with heavy loss.

The lancers were more fortunate in their venture. As they swept past the right flank of the Forty-Second and Forty-Fourth, which were standing in line close to the eastern margin of the Brussels road, they were so closely intermingled with the Brunswick Hussars and Belgians that the British at first mistook them for the Allied cavalry. A few old soldiers did indeed recognise them as enemies and open fire, but were sternly repressed by Pack; and the lancers, then wheeling about, charged down upon the rear of the British regiments. The Forty-Second, having had a closer view of the cavalry than the Forty-

Fourth, realised their danger and began to form square, but, before the two flank-companies could run in to close the rear face, the lancers overtook them and, by the impetus of their charge, some few of them crashed into the mass of the battalion.

For a moment there was some confusion. The senior officers sprang forward to rally the Highlanders, and in a few minutes the colonel, second and third in command were dead. Then the flank-companies closed in, the square was completed, and the lancers, who had at first broken in, found themselves imprisoned and were bayoneted or taken to a man. The rest were driven off by the musketry of the remaining faces of the square with very heavy loss. Meanwhile the colonel of the Forty-Fourth, seeing that there was no time to form square, faced his rear rank about, and, waiting till the enemy was within close range, gave them a volley which emptied many saddles and effectually checked the rest. One little knot of daring Frenchmen, however, made a gallant dash for the colours, which were as gallantly defended; and, though the precious silk was actually torn by the point of a French lance, not a fragment became a trophy to the enemy.

Meanwhile the bulk of the lancers fled round the left flank of the battalion, receiving a volley from the light company as they passed, and were saluted by another discharge from the front rank before they finally disappeared. Let it be added that Colonel Galbois of the 6th French Lancers received a bullet in the chest during this encounter, but remained in the saddle and commanded his regiment two days later at Waterloo. Never did British soldiers bear themselves better, and never were they matched against nobler foemen.

On the whole, Ney's great attack had failed. He had been completely repulsed at every point to east of the Brussels road; and his attempts to turn the British left flank had been steadily foiled by the Riflemen, [9] who, though driven by artillery from their little citadel at Thyle, continued to defend the Namur road with the greatest obstinacy. Only in Bossu Wood, which seems to have swallowed up the bulk

---

9. They had been reinforced by a Brunswick battalion, so raw that they could not be restrained from firing in all directions, and chiefly at their friends the Riflemen.

10. It is exceedingly difficult to follow the movements of the French infantry in this action. Soye's brigade of Jerome's division was in Bossu Wood, but Bauduin's was free to advance between the wood and the Brussels road. Of Foy's division, one regiment of Jamin's brigade was covering the re-formation of Bachelu's division, but the other should have been advancing parallel with Bauduin's brigade; while Gauthier's brigade, albeit repulsed at the outset, should have been re-forming or re-formed in rear of Jamin. Apparently all movements of the infantry, (cont. next page),

of Jerome's division, [10] were the French making progress in spite of the thickness of the undergrowth. At this point indeed the resistance of the Netherlanders, as was pardonable in young troops which had been roughly handled, was beginning to grow weak; and, as the Forty-Second, Forty-Fourth and Seventy-Ninth had suffered very heavily, being always under the fire of the French artillery, Wellington's situation was not of the securest.

But, on the other hand, Ney also was in trouble. Soult's message had arrived reiterating the order to march upon the right flank of Blücher, and warning him that the fate of France was in his hands; and, as if in mockery, there came to his hands almost simultaneously a message carried by the chief of d'Erlon's staff, reporting that by the emperor's order the 1st Corps was on its way to the battlefield of Ligny. Furious with rage, Ney sent a peremptory order to d'Erlon to return at once, and calling to him Kellermann, told him that the time was come for a great effort, and that he must hurl his cavalry at the British and gallop over them.

Possibly the marshal forgot that three out of four brigades of Kellermann's cavalry corps were at Liberchies, and only one brigade present at Frasnes, [11] and was under the impression that he was about to launch thirty-five hundred men upon the Allied line instead of eight hundred. Be that as it may, Kellermann demurred to the order, pointing out that a single brigade could do little against twenty-five thousand men. "What matter?" cried Ney. "Charge with whatever you have got. Gallop over them. I'll support you with all the cavalry that I have on the spot. Off with you! I say, off with you!"

Kellermann thereupon went to the head of Guiton's brigade and led them at a smart trot down the road; while the French batteries redoubled their fire upon the British infantry. Arrived at the summit of the plateau north of the Gemioncourt rivulet, he increased his front to a column of squadrons at twice deploying distance, and advanced at a gallop, hurrying his men into action before they could perceive their danger. The first attack was delivered on the east of the road

except in the wood, were suspended during the attack of the cavalry; presumably because the troops to east of the wood dared not advance until their left flank was cleared. It seems probable that these last were for long checked at the re-entrant angle where the northern end of the wood joins the road.

11. Siborne says that the whole of L'Héritier's division was at Frasnes; Houssaye says that Guiton's brigade only was engaged, and this is confirmed by the reports both of Ney and of Kellermann. The latter indeed said that he did not know where L'Héritier's division was.

against the Forty-Second and Forty-Fourth, which, unable to see anything over the tall stalks of the rye in June 16. which they stood, were warned of the coming wrath by the inrush of their skirmishers. By this time both battalions had been reduced to little more than half of their original strength, but they formed two tiny squares with perfect steadiness and awaited the shock.

The horses of the *cuirassiers*, after a rapid advance of over a mile, the latter part of the distance through thick corn as high as their withers, were doubtless somewhat blown; but their riders pressed them gallantly on almost to the points of the British bayonets. Then at last the red-coats drew trigger, and the leading squadron, broken and shattered by the fire, swerved away and disappeared. The other squadrons followed them in wave upon wave, only to meet with the same fate; and then, rallying, they renewed their onset upon two or more different faces of the squares, striving desperately but in vain to break into the hedge of bayonets. Some of the rear squadrons, meanwhile, dashed straight on by the road and parallel to it upon Quatre Bras and the Highlanders who were aligned to east of it.

"Ninety-Second, don't fire till I tell you!" shouted Wellington; and, waiting until the enemy were within thirty yards, he gave the word, when a withering volley sent the daring horsemen back in confusion.

The *cuirassiers* then retired to rally [12] under the shelter of the southern slope of the ridge, leaving the artillery to play upon the squares. Being reinforced by Piré's *chasseurs* and lancers, they presently renewed the attack. Once again there was a wild rush upon Quatre Bras and once again it was shattered by the Ninety-Second, though a few brave horsemen made their way into the village and one French officer was actually shot in rear of the Highlanders. But the principal onslaught was, as before, upon the Forty-Second and Forty-Fourth, which were fairly hemmed in and hidden by a mixed multitude of chasseurs, lancers, and *cuirassiers*, but nevertheless stood indomitably firm and refused to be broken.

At last Picton, weary of waiting for the Netherlandish cavalry to come to the front, formed the First Royals and Twenty-Eighth in one solid column of companies and advanced with them from the Namur

12. It is extremely difficult to discover how many distinct attacks were delivered by the French cavalry. Houssaye treats them all as one; Siborne treats them as two; but judging from the narratives of the British regiments in *Waterloo Letters* I conceive that there were four, one of cuirassiers only, a second of cuirassiers supported by Piré's division, and a third and fourth, in one or both of which Lefebvre-Desnoëtte's division, or a part of it, took some share.

road into the thick of the French horse upon the right of the Forty-Fourth. Halting when he had reached a position from which he could bring a flanking fire to bear in favour of the Forty-Fourth, he suddenly formed both regiments into one square; and, the Thirty-Second and Seventy-Ninth advancing likewise in the same formation to the south of the Royals and Twenty-Eighth, the division made up a cluster of five squares drawn up more or less chequerwise for mutual support.

At the same time Best's Hanoverian Brigade came forward to line the Namur road, which it did with three battalions, the fourth being pushed somewhat in advance. Against the new squares of red-coats the French turned with undiminished spirit and valour. Unable to see their enemy owing to the height of the rye, some of Piré's troopers fixed their lances in the ground close to the various squares, and upon these marks their comrades charged again and again with desperate but unavailing hardihood. There appears to have been little method in their attacks. There was no crash of squadron after squadron upon one given point, but an endless swirl of horsemen round and round the squares, which, though slightly thinned by occasional lance-thrusts, maintained eternally their deadly rolling fire. Scores of men and horses were brought down; and at length the French horsemen were again called off, to be rallied and re-formed.

Once more the French guns opened on the squares, and, worse still, the French sharp-shooters crept up and began to pour a destructive fire upon them. Perforce British skirmishers had to go forward to meet them; but with so little ammunition that they were at great disadvantage. At length the last round was exhausted, and Pack recalled the skirmishers to the squares; but, before the order could be executed, the *cuirassiers* and lancers were upon them. Forming into columns of fours the little band charged through the horsemen, reached the Forty-Fourth and lay down under the bayonets, the square being so hotly assailed at the moment that it could not open its ranks even to admit friends. The French commanders, evidently endeavouring to improve their tactics, marshalled their men for a simultaneous attack upon three sides of the square of the Royals and Twenty-Eighth.

Picton uttered not a word except "Twenty-Eighth, remember Egypt," and the charge was beaten off, as had been all previous charges, with heavy loss to the enemy. Thereupon the old disorder began afresh, and the attack degenerated into a confusion of galloping swarms in and out of the squares. At one point, however, it was at last successful, for a party of lancers surprised Best's advanced Hanoverian battalion when deployed in line, and practically destroyed it. Heartened by this victory the lancers tried to cross the Namur road, but were driven back in confusion by the fire of the remaining battalions which were concealed in a ditch by the highway. Then for the third time the French cavalry was drawn off to re-form; and the red-coats were left to the mercy of the cannon and sharpshooters of the enemy.

The Forty-Second and Forty-Fourth were now formed into a single square under the personal command of Pack; but, having little ammunition left, they and the Seventy-Ninth were reduced almost to the limits of their endurance. Happily at this moment came up two brigades of Alten's division, Colin Halkett's British and Kielmansegge's Hanoverians, the former of which was directed by Picton to move down through Bossu Wood and fall upon the French left, and the latter to reinforce the Riflemen on the extreme Allied left. Entering the wood, Halkett encountered an *aide-de-camp* sent by Pack, who represented that there were few cartridges left in his brigade, and that unless speedily supported he could no longer hold his position.

Detaching the Sixty-Ninth to the help of Pack, Halkett led the rest of his brigade into the wood just in time to stop the Brunswickers, who were on the point of abandoning it. The Brunswickers were not without excuse, for the bulk of the Netherlanders were by this time streaming away in flight along the road to Nivelles. [13] By a few hard words, aided by the presence of his own brigade, Halkett induced them to rally in a ditch which ran across the narrowest part of the wood, and galloped forward to the ground overlooking Gemioncourt to reconnoitre.

Perceiving below him a large corps of cavalry forming by detachments, and seeing the French cannon reopen fire, he despatched an *aide-de-camp* to warn the Sixty-Ninth to form square, and received an answer that his orders were obeyed. The French cavalry, reinforced ap-

---

13. In spite of the statements of Le Bas and Wommersom, the concurrence of testimony as to the flight of the Netherlanders at this time is so strong that I cannot overlook it. The private *Journal* of Colonel James Stanhope who came up with the 1st Guards says: "Soon after passing Nivelles we met a great many wounded men going to the rear with ten times their number to take care of them, which did not strike me as a good specimen of the first trial of our Allies." Such a witness had no object in saying what was untrue, and he confirms the general reports of other British writers.

14. Or by some part of it. See Houssaye, *Waterloo*, (republished by Leonaur as *1815, Waterloo*). I do not see how the French cavalry could have come forward again without reinforcement: particularly as we are told that the cuirassiers took part in every one of the attacks, and only two regiments of cuirassiers were present.

parently by Lefebvre-Desnoëtte's division, [14] was in fact massing for a fourth and final attack which was to be supported by infantry. Bossu Wood had by this time been nearly cleared of the Allied battalions, so that Bauduin's, Jamin's and Gauthier's brigades were able to advance, some of them in the open, most of them, it should seem, within the wood itself; and Ney had ordered two batteries of artillery to advance along a ride close to the eastern margin of the wood and running parallel with it, so as to emerge at the right moment from the wood into the plain and prepare the way for the onslaught of the infantry.

Wellington had been temporarily absent from Quatre Bras when Halkett came up, but sent an *aide-de-camp* to ask if Sir Colin could follow the original instructions given by Picton. He was answered that it seemed unsafe to leave the Brunswickers unsupported until more troops should come up. Halkett's brigade was therefore disposed, apparently, so as at once to take pressure off Picton's right and to maintain the defence of the north-eastern angle of the wood. The whole were echeloned, [15] it seems, to west of the Brussels road, the Sixty-Ninth, together with two guns of Lloyd's battery which had just arrived, foremost, and the Thirtieth next to them.

As they reached their appointed ground they began to form square, in obedience to Halkett's warning, when the Prince of Orange galloped up and asked them what they were about, as there was no fear of any further attack by cavalry. Pursuant to the prince's command the two battalions deployed into line, and the two guns were presently recalled to join the rest of their battery just south of the farm of Quatre Bras. Cleeves's and Kuhlmann's batteries of the German Legion appeared shortly afterwards, whereupon Lloyd's took post on the west side of the road, Cleeves's on the east side, and Kuhlmann's midway between them.

Shortly afterwards the French cavalry came up the road to their fourth attack, and catching sight of the Thirty-Third, which was moving in column of companies through the rye on the highest point of the plateau, galloped upon them. The battalion formed square, whereupon the baffled horsemen, perceiving the Sixty-Ninth in a hollow below, wheeled round and charged down upon them. The Sixty-Ninth being, through the folly of the Prince of Orange, deployed, made shift to throw itself into square and, apparently, would have suc-

15. It is most difficult to discover the position of Halkett's brigade. Amid all the libraries that have been written on the campaign of Waterloo it is almost impossible to ascertain so simple a point as this.

ceeded had not the captain of the grenadier company wheeled the two right-hand companies about in order to fire, instead of closing the face of the square.

In a moment the horsemen were in the middle of them. The two companies were destroyed, the rest were partly broken, the only remaining colour of the battalion was captured, one hundred and fifty men were killed and wounded, and the remainder saved themselves by taking refuge under the bayonets of the Forty-Second and Forty-Fourth. [16] Flushed with success, the cavalry turned upon the Thirtieth, which, however, having had time to form square, beat them off with a steadiness which earned warm praise from Picton. Some of the *cuirassiers* then essayed a last desperate attempt upon Quatre Bras, but were shattered to pieces by Cleeves's guns; and the survivors fled in headlong panic along the Brussels road, infecting with their fright some of the infantry as they passed, and carrying dismay even to Charleroi and beyond. [17]

Nevertheless the danger of Wellington's situation was never greater than at this moment. The Sixty-Ninth was for the time dispersed; the Seventy-Third, upon the sight of the cavalry approaching them, had run into the thicket; [18] and now the French batteries concealed in the wood opened fire with deadly effect upon the Thirty-Third. After enduring the trial for a short time the colonel deployed the battalion, and, covered by a regiment of Brunswick cavalry, moved towards a battalion of Brunswick infantry which was heavily engaged in the re-entrant angle of the wood near Quatre Bras. A cry rose that the cavalry was again approaching, and the Thirty-Third rushed into the wood and dispersed. The Thirtieth appears to have altered its formation and stood firm, [19] but, with this exception, Halkett's brigade was for the time out of action; and the French cavalry returned to its old task of rushing round the squares of Pack's brigade. These still held their ground with noble tenacity, but Bossu Wood was practically lost to the Allies for the moment.

---

16. The colonel, who was killed at Waterloo, told Captain Rudyard of Lloyd's battery that the battalion was saved by the fire of a battalion of Guards (*Waterloo Letters*); but it is, I think, impossible that the Guards were so early on the field.

17. I conceive that these fugitives were the 3rd Léger of Bauduin's brigade and possibly the 93rd Line of Gauthier's brigade. The 3rd lost not a single officer killed or wounded, and the 93rd only two officers.

18. Morris. *Recollections of Military Service*. (Republished by Leonaur as *Sergeant Morris of the 73rd*).

19. *Life of Sir William Gomm*.

Its eastern border was full of British troops, but these were dispersed in the undergrowth, some of them no doubt glad to find themselves in a safe place and unwilling to leave it, but all, including the officers, absolutely lost, without an idea in which direction they were moving or ought to move, how they were to assemble themselves and what they should do when assembled. The French, on the other hand, were pushing on to the Nivelles road with every prospect of turning Wellington's right; and, if they should succeed in doing this, the day would be lost.

Happily at this moment the division of Guards, followed by two Brunswick battalions and a Brunswick battery, approached Quatre Bras, much fatigued after a march of fifteen hours. The Prince of Orange, in a high state of excitement, galloped out to meet them, and encountering Lord Saltoun at the head of the light companies of the First Guards, ordered him to strike south-eastward into the western side of Bossu Wood. Saltoun, unable to see any enemy, asked where the French were to be found.

"If you do not like to undertake it," answered the foolish prince, excitedly, "I'll find some one who will." Saltoun, who had served with distinction through the campaigns of Coruna, Walcheren, Vitoria, the Pyrenees, and Southern France, quietly repeated his question and, upon obtaining a reasonable reply, formed his line of skirmishers and entered the wood. Guided only by the sound of the enemy's musketry, these pressed forward steadily, while the Prince of Orange, utterly ignorant of his business, hurried the succeeding companies in pairs, as they came up, close on the heels of Saltoun. Unable to see anything, these supporting companies could only fire where they could hear firing, and this undoubtedly caused some loss among Saltoun's men.

However, their advance certainly checked that of the French on the western side of the wood; and meanwhile Lloyd's battery, moving. forward from Quatre Bras, engaged the two French batteries on the eastern margin of the wood. After a murderous duel which cost Lloyd several men and two complete teams, he succeeded not only in silencing them but in driving back a French column which attempted to debouch from the trees in that quarter. But farther to the north two French columns, following not far upon the heels of the defeated cuirassiers, had turned north-eastward out of the wood upon Quatre Bras, one of them occupying the house and garden of La Bergerie. Sir Edward Barnes therefore placed himself at the head of the Ninety-Second, which charged the head of the leading column and drove it back into the garden. Under a murderous flanking fire from the second column the Highlanders then assaulted the building and its enclosures, cleared the enemy from it after a desperate encounter, and fairly drove the French down before them along the margin between wood and road until they came under the fire of the French guns posted on the hill opposite Gemioncourt. Then at last they withdrew into the wood for shelter, whence they retired, with ranks terribly thinned, to Quatre Bras.

Not long afterwards the Second battalion of the First Guards, after not much less than an hour of confused fighting, penetrated to the extreme south-western angle of Bossu Wood, with its companies naturally much intermixed and its order in great measure lost. By that time the bulk of Halkett's brigade had been rallied and reposted level with the Gemioncourt Brook, with the two new Brunswick battalions somewhat in advance of them; and, when the Guards emerged into the open ground, they could see the Thirty-Third behind the shelter of a hedge to their left rear. They were however received by so heavy a fire of musketry and artillery when they showed themselves, that they withdrew again to a hollow formed by a rill that runs north and south through the wood, though even then they suffered some loss from heavy branches cut off by the French round-shot.

Here, being joined by their Third battalion, the First Guards advanced again into the open between the wood and the Brussels road, having rallied to them a number of lost men of Halkett's brigade, while Byng's brigade came and began to form up on their right. The deployment was in process and the Brunswick battalion was moving down to form on the left of Maitland's brigade, when the French *cuirassiers* made a dash upon the left flank of the First Guards. The men instantly ran back to line the ditch at the edge of the wood while the Brunswickers formed square; and the *cuirassiers*, met by the fire of the Guards in front and of the Brunswickers in flank, were driven back with very heavy loss. Nevertheless all Maitland's attempts to make further progress and to storm the French battery were frustrated by the steadiness of the French infantry.

On the Allied left a resolute attempt of Bachelu to turn Wellington's left was foiled, after much hard fighting, by the Rifles, with the support of two Hanoverian battalions; and soon after sunset all French attacks ceased, and their cavalry vanished from the ground. Ney had, in fact, withdrawn all his troops to Frasnes; and at nine o'clock, as the darkness thickened, Wellington established his line of picquets from

Petit Pierrepont, through Gemioncourt to Pireaumont, over against the outposts of Ney. Thus was recovered, after a struggle of six hours, the original position (the farm of Grand Pierrepont excepted) which had been occupied by Perponcher in the morning.

Few engagements are more difficult to follow and to understand than the Battle of Quatre Bras. It is impossible, in the first place, to say definitely what numbers of the Allies were in action at any given moment after the first hour or even half-hour. Fresh troops were constantly coming up from beginning to end of the fight, and, though many authors have tried to settle the hour at which this or that brigade or division arrived on the ground, the data upon which they have reckoned are so uncertain that no reliance can be placed upon them. The hours stated by various actors who have left narratives of the struggle are, again, so contradictory that any endeavour to reconcile them is hopeless.

It is also extremely hard to discover exactly what force of cavalry was at the disposal of Ney. Some narratives [20] on the side of the Allies state that Roussel's *cuirassiers* were present at the end of the day, but did not charge; and indeed the ubiquity of the cuirassiers, as portrayed by the concurrence of many English narrators, would seem to demand the presence of more than one brigade of this particular description of cavalry. The constant mention of lancers also would seem to imply that those of Lefebvre-Desnoëttes as well as those of Piré were among the squadrons which harassed Picton's battalions through so many hours. Yet, according to the list of casualties, not a single officer of Roussel's brigade and only two officers of Lefebvre-Desnoëttes's command were touched on the 16th of June. The height of the rye-stalks, the veiling of the French right by Hutte Wood as of the Allied right by Bossu Wood, and the undulations of the ground evidently made accurate observation impracticable.

The only certain fact that can be adduced is that Ney began the fight with about fifteen thousand infantry, eighteen hundred cavalry, and thirty-eight guns against about seven thousand infantry, with no cavalry and sixteen guns; and that when the battle ended Ney's force had probably been augmented by more than a thousand horse, whereas Wellington's had been swelled by the arrival, at different periods, of some twenty-two thousand men and forty-two guns. Of course

---

20. *E.g.* Siborne's and the French *Témoin oculaire*. See *The Battle of Waterloo*, by a Near Observer. Siborne also credits Ney with the whole of Héritier's cavalry division instead of with Guiton's brigade only.

the value of the troops that from first to last came under Wellington's command during the day varied very greatly, but, so far as bare numbers go, the figures are roughly as above stated. That Wellington was in constant peril was due to the facts, first, that every successive reinforcement as it came up had to bear the full weight of the French attack, which had already overwhelmed its predecessors; and secondly, that he had no British cavalry present. For these disadvantages no one can be held responsible but himself.

The conduct of the troops of all nations in the field, without exception, varied greatly. Taking first the Netherlanders, to whom without dispute belongs the credit of occupying and defending the position of Quatre Bras in the first instance, it appears that the 27th Chasseurs, the 5th Militia and the 2nd Nassau Light Infantry, all three of them, lost heavily in killed and wounded; but of the wounded a very large proportion were but slightly hurt, and the 27th and the 5th both show a discreditable number of men missing. The losses of the seven remaining battalions, so far as they are returned, were slight indeed, except in one instance, so trifling as to prove that those units took only a minute share in the action. [21]

On the other hand, Van Merlen's two cavalry regiments seem to have behaved better, though here again the proportion of slightly wounded is unduly large; and Stevenaart's battery of artillery, which lost all its officers and fifty killed or wounded, [22] must have behaved not only well but heroically. The casualties of the Netherlanders, all told, amounted to a thousand and fifty-eight, of which nearly three hundred were missing and nearly four hundred slightly wounded, leaving a balance of only four to five hundred killed or seriously hurt. For a total force of nine thousand present, most of them for the entire day, such a tale of casualties does not suggest very strenuous resistance or very serious loss; and, in spite of all that has been written in defence of their countrymen by Netherlandish authors, the contemporary judgment which threw the brunt of the day's work upon the British and Germans must stand as confirmed.

Nevertheless it would be unfair to judge too harshly troops so

21. One battalion of Militia is omitted from the return altogether, which, unless it were dissolved, is rather remarkable.
22. The figure given by Le Bas and Wommersom in their text is 1 officer and 28 men killed, 2 officers and 83 men wounded, making 114 casualties out of 119 present. This does not agree with the return printed in vol. iii., where the figures are 1 officer and 6 men killed, 2 officers and 13 men severely wounded, 3 officers and 25 men slightly wounded, 14 men missing. Total casualties 63.

lately raised for a sovereign so newly appointed; and at all events the highest praise must be given to the Netherlandish generals, Constant and Perponcher. The like cannot be said of the Prince of Orange, who succeeded in destroying one British battalion, and did his best to destroy three more. His courage was unquestionable, but, considered as a general officer, he can be described only as a meddlesome and mischievous encumbrance.

Of the Brunswickers, those that were rallied by Halkett were not seen at their best, but the rest appear to have conducted themselves well, indeed, for young soldiers, admirably. Their losses amounted to nearly eight hundred and fifty, one quarter of them missing; two battalions having each about one hundred casualties and a third close upon two hundred. The Hanoverians also displayed commendable steadiness in spite of the misfortune which overtook one of their battalions. Their casualties well exceeded six hundred. Of the British the battalions of Picton's division rose to the highest level of excellence attained by British infantry, their constancy under repeated devastation by artillery and incessant attacks of cavalry being superb.

The Guards also maintained worthily their high reputation, being thrown into action at a very trying moment after a march of twenty-six miles, with shaken troops on every side of them. The casualties among them and the battalions of Picton's division were heavy. In the First Guards the Second and Third battalions lost over five hundred out of two thousand rank and file. In Pack's brigade, the Royals had over two hundred killed and wounded, and Forty-Second and Ninety-Second each over two hundred and eighty, representing in the case of the two last not far from one -half of their numbers.

In Kempt's brigade the Thirty-Second had very nearly two hundred casualties, and the Seventy-Ninth just over three hundred. Halkett's brigade, excepting the Sixty-Ninth, escaped more lightly; but it must be frankly confessed that as a body they behaved ill, though Halkett himself selected only the Thirty-third for reproach. But they were raw young soldiers, remnants of Graham's force, and were hardly equal to the severe trial of remaining stationary under the fire of cannon, varied only by occasional charges of cavalry; and the Prince of Orange's disastrous interference with their formation was not calculated to inspire them with confidence. Nevertheless, their behaviour was a blot upon the general conduct of the red-coats. The total losses of the British amounted to close upon twenty-three hundred, among whom the missing did June 16. not amount to forty. The casualties of the entire force of the Allies reached the total of forty-eight hundred exactly.

The losses of the French are stated at forty-one to forty-two hundred, which is probably not far from correct. The distribution of loss, so far as can be gathered from the only source of information the casualty-list of officers was almost startlingly unequal. In Bachelu's division there fell altogether thirty-six officers, of whom fourteen belonged to the 61st of the Line, five to the 72nd, and seventeen to the 108th. On the whole this division suffered severely. In Jerome's division, the number was the same, thirty-six, but of these twenty-seven belonged to the 1st of the Line and six to the 2nd, while in Bauduin's brigade only three officers were killed or wounded in 1st Light and not one in the 3rd Light.

From this it is tolerably certain that Bauduin's brigade was but slightly engaged, and that the 3rd Light ran away in the panic caused by the flight of the *cuirassiers*. In Foy's division eight officers only fell in Gauthier's brigade, whereas in Jamin's no fewer than twenty-nine were killed and wounded in the 4th Light alone, besides fifteen of the 100th of the Line. Foy states his losses at seven to eight hundred, but it is manifest that the brunt fell on one regiment principally; and, when one reflects on the small share of the work which was evidently done by Bauduin, one cannot but be filled with admiration for the persistent gallantry of the remainder of the French infantry and in particular of the 1st Line and the 4th Light.

Not all the endeavours of the Guards could avail to recover more ground than had been held by the Netherlanders in the morning; and this is no small tribute to the tenacity of their enemies. Not less remarkable was the inexhaustible courage and energy of Piré's lancers and of Guiton's *cuirassiers*, who suffered terribly in their attacks upon the British infantry. Here, however, there is again an irregularity in the distribution of the casualties which is difficult to explain. The 5th Lancers lost ten officers, the 6th eleven; but the 1st Chasseurs of the same division lost only two and the 6th Chasseurs not one. In Guiton's brigade there fell of the 8th Cuirassiers alone thirteen officers, but of the 11th Cuirassiers only four. Lastly, in Lefebvre-Desnoëttes' division two officers of the lancers of the Guard were wounded, but not one of the Chasseurs. The conclusion would seem to be that Ney at no time threw the whole of his forces into the fight, which is one more testimony to the bravery and endeavour of those that were actually engaged.

A great deal has been written, after the event, of Ney's shortcomings in the morning of the 16th, his failure to assemble his infantry betimes at Quatre Bras, and his omission to ascertain the strength of the Allies by a reconnaissance in force. Such criticism is easy, but it takes no account of the false view of the entire situation which had been held up to the marshal by his master Napoleon. Setting aside his unsurpassable moral and physical courage, Ney had never been much more than an exceedingly skilful tactician in the field, being content with his chief's direction in higher matters. He had only joined the army after the actual opening of the campaign, consequently he knew nothing about his command, and little more than had been vouchsafed to him in Napoleon's first letter about the plan of operations.

The emperor had given him plainly to understand that the road to Brussels was open, and probably the road to Gembloux also. Ney naturally presumed that his chief knew best, and he no doubt laid himself out for a quiet day in which to settle down to his work before the march to Brussels at nightfall. Napoleon had in fact fallen into the error which he had so frequently rebuked in his subordinates—*il se faisait des tableaux*, he had conjured up imaginary pictures of the situation. He had made up his mind that both of the Allied armies were retreating, when he discovered first that the Prussians were standing firm and ready to accept battle.

For this he was more or less prepared. He had his two wings and his reserve ready for such a contingency, and welcomed the opportunity of annihilating one army while in isolation from the other. Once again he conjured up a picture of forty thousand Prussians only before him, whereas there proved to be eighty thousand. For this also he was in a measure ready, for he had announced that, when necessary, he should weaken one wing to strengthen the other. He accordingly proceeded first to summon Ney's entire force to him, and meanwhile took d'Erlon's corps from him bodily. But, as the proceedings of the day developed, it became apparent that the French army was saddled, not with one pitched battle, but with two. Both wings were busily engaged at one and the same time, which was contrary to all of Napoleon's principles and plans, and the reserve was reduced practically to d'Erlon's corps, which was needed and clamoured for equally by Napoleon and by Ney.

The not unnatural result was that d'Erlon spent the day marching backwards and forwards between Ligny and Quatre Bras, and did not finally settle down at Frasnes until night had put an end to the fighting everywhere. His corps thrown in upon either battlefield would undoubtedly have secured a decided success for the emperor; and d'Erlon has been much blamed for obeying Ney's command to return from St. Amand. We have seen enough of this officer during the campaign in the Pyrenees to know that he was not a man to commit himself upon any side so long as he could find a safe way in the middle; and it is therefore not surprising that he should have acted as he did. But the key to his irresolution and to Ney's apathy was undoubtedly Napoleon's misjudgement of the whole situation.

Napoleon's first word on the 16th was, practically, "There will be no fighting today"; his second, "I shall fight a battle today, and shall need all my reserves to make it decisive"; whereas events proved that he was destined to fight two severe battles, one of them successful, the other unsuccessful, but neither decisive. A little more tactical skill on the part of Blücher would have made both of them unsuccessful, and then his plan of campaign would have been ruined. Even as it was, his losses certainly not far short of thirteen thousand men incurred as they were for no final result, threatened to work havoc with his operations, for it was certain that two more such engagements would bring his army to a standstill. Altogether the 16th of June was a bad day for Napoleon, and chiefly through his own fault. The fact is that he overrated the effect of his prestige, and omitted from his calculations the important factor that the two generals opposed to him were not afraid of him.

Still less did he bethink him that one of the two was a commander whom his own generals were afraid to meet. But for the unpleasant memories of Peninsular battles Ney would probably have attacked earlier, and taken Quatre Bras before Picton's division could have arrived in time to save it. The events of the 16th of June turned, it may be said, chiefly on the singular circumstance that, at any rate for that day, Wellington's name inspired greater awe into the French than Napoleon's into the Allies.

The Lines are Drawn

The armies of Napoleon, Wellington and Ney were all of them too much exhausted to move on the evening of the 16th; but the Prussians had no choice but to retire. Some of their Ist and IInd Corps had been very severely handled and were to some extent demoralised. Fugitives swarmed along the road to Liége, and, though many were turned back by Prussian officers, it was reckoned that from eight to ten thousand forsook their colours and pursued their way in no sort of order. Some hundreds of Prussian marauders and bad characters, indeed, even found their way to Brussels, where, among other depredations, they stole several horses belonging to British officers. [1]

On the other hand, the actual losses in action did not exceed six thousand, of which only a small proportion were prisoners, and the guns captured by the French little exceeded twenty. Two of Ziethen's brigades and one of Thielmann's had firmly arrested the French advances at Brye and before Sombreffe; and Thielmann, whose corps had been little engaged, finally stood fast about Sombreffe till past ten o'clock. Gneisenau, who was left in command owing to Blücher's injuries, had at first given provisional orders for retreat northward to Tilly; but he was much inclined to fall back upon Liége, and it was only after a warm discussion between him, Blücher and Grolmann that he at last gave way to them, and early in the morning of the 17th issued the final command for retreat to Wavre.

This decision has been rightly styled the turning point of the campaign, and, so far as Blücher and Grolmann were concerned, it certainly signified their fixed intention to stand by their Allies. Gneisenau

---

1 Jackson. *Notes and Reminiscences of a Staff Officer*, (republished by Leonaur as *With Wellington's Staff at Waterloo*).

was influenced by no such motive; and indeed the movement by no means necessarily bound him to co-operation with Wellington.

A retreat upon Liege, if carried out by the Roman road, would not have been the safest of operations with a Napoleon within striking distance, whereas by retiring northward to Louvain he could strike a second and far securer line of communication with the Rhine Provinces by Maastricht and Aix-la-Chapelle. Headquarters for the night were fixed at Mellery, and at daybreak of the 17th the whole army marched upon Wavre, where Pirch I.'s corps took up its bivouac to south at Ste. Anne and Aisemont, Ziethen's to west at Bierges, and Thielmann's to north at La Bavette. Bülow at the same time was called in to Dion-le-Mont, about three miles south-east of Wavre, where he arrived at ten o'clock at night. Thus the Prussian army effected its retirement without molestation, and on the night of the 17th was concentrated in full force and by no means in bad heart. The only thing which the Prussian staff had omitted to do was to inform Wellington of their retreat.

At Quatre Bras the British cavalry continued to stream in through the evening and night; and by daybreak of the 17th all six of the brigades, one regiment excepted, had arrived, bringing the total of the force up to forty-five thousand men. Two *aides-de-camp* had been sent to Wellington by Gneisenau in the course of the 16th, the first of whom was wounded near Pireaumont and never delivered his message, while the second brought the news that, though no great success was to be expected as the outcome of the fight, the Prussians hoped to hold their ground till nightfall. Relying upon this assurance the duke rested at Genappe for the night, returning to Quatre Bras soon after daylight.

There was some firing among the most advanced skirmishers upon both sides, which after a time died away. As there was still no information from the Prussians and it was therefore uncertain whether the next march was to be in advance or in retreat, Wellington soon after six o'clock sent a staff officer, Sir Alexander Gordon, escorted by a troop of the Tenth Hussars, towards Ligny. This party, after driving in a French picquet about Marbais, turned north and, meeting General Ziethen, who was directing the movements of the Prussian rear-guard, ascertained from him the truth respecting the events of the 16th. When Gordon returned with his report, the duke looked meaningly at Müffling, who, conscious of his own good faith, explained that the Prussian *aide-decamp*, who had been wounded at Pireaumont, had probably been sent to convey this very news.

Wellington, instantly pacified, proceeded to discuss what should be done. At present he knew only that Blücher had retreated upon Wavre and that Bülow's corps had not been engaged; and the only course appeared to be to retire to some position level with Wavre, and to regulate his future operations by the reports that should reach him from Blücher. After some hesitation the duke decided to let the men cook and eat their breakfasts before moving; and at nine o'clock a Prussian officer arrived to report Blücher's resolution of concentrating at Wavre, and to ascertain Wellington's intentions. The duke answered that he should retire to Mont St. Jean, where, if supported by one Prussian corps, he should accept battle.

The retreat of Pirch I. and Ziethen, astonishing to I say, was unobserved on the French left; but on the right Pajol's patrols reported at half-past two in the morning that the Prussians were in motion, and Pajol without delay sent two regiments in pursuit along the road to Namur. Stragglers and lost units, including a stray squadron and a stray battery, induced the French hussars to follow this false track, and at five o'clock Pajol reported definitely that the enemy was retreating along the road to Namur and Liége. Pursuing his way for some hours, however, he began to doubt if he were right, and at noon, upon the information of some peasants, he turned northwards by a by-road towards Louvain. Berton's brigade of Exelmans's cavalry corps also followed the road to Namur for a short distance, but soon turned towards Gembloux, where at nine o'clock in the morning it came upon Thielmann's whole corps halted for rest. Exelmans himself presently came up, but contented himself with watching the Prussians and sending a despatch, rather late, to report that he was doing so.

Meanwhile, at about seven o'clock, the emperor received Pajol's message above mentioned; and nearly at the same time his *aide-de-camp*, Flahault, returned from Quatre Bras and gave an account of what had passed there. Deciding not to issue any definite orders, Napoleon gave Ney notice that he was proceeding to Brye, and that, if there were any trouble with the British army, he would attack it in flank while Ney assailed it in front, so as to compel it to yield up Quatre Bras. The rest of the day, he added, would be spent in collecting stragglers and replenishing stores. At nine o'clock, accordingly, he left Fleurus for the battlefield of Ligny, where he inspected his troops and visited the wounded.

Here letters reached him from Ney, from Pajol and from Exelmans. The first set forth that the Allied troops at Quatre Bras were an army and not a mere rear-guard; the second reported the capture of guns and prisoners at Mazy on the Namur road; and the third announced that Exelmans was marching with his cavalry corps upon Gembloux in pursuit of the Prussians.[2] Thereupon Napoleon decided to divide his army, and delivered his final instructions to that end. To Grouchy he handed over Teste's division of Lobau's corps, Vandamme's and Gérard's corps complete, and the four cavalry divisions of Pajol and Exelmans, with instructions to proceed with them to Gembloux. From that centre the Marshal was to explore in the direction of Namur and Maastricht, pursue the enemy and discover his movements. Napoleon himself would meanwhile proceed to Quatre Bras; and the line of communications, which was to be well guarded, would be by the paved road to Namur.

In any case, Grouchy was to keep his infantry in a compact body with several avenues of retreat. One sentence ran:

> It is important to discover what Blücher and Wellington mean to do, and whether they intend to unite their armies to cover Brussels and Liege by trying their luck in another battle.[3]

According to the purport of these instructions, as I read them, Grouchy's mission was to be one principally of reconnaissance and exploration. The emperor repeats twice in the course of a few lines that he wishes to penetrate his enemy's intentions. With this object, chiefly, as the text appears to indicate, Grouchy was to pursue the Prussians, and, though he was to start at Gembloux, he was directed particularly to make good the ground towards Namur, and indeed to cause that line to be occupied by National Guards in case it had been evacuated by the Prussians. This shows plainly that Napoleon was still wedded to his original idea, confirmed as it was to some extent by Pajol's reports, that Blücher had retreated eastwards.

In this case Grouchy might have to deal with a strong rear-guard

---

2. Houssaye: *Waterloo.* I think it too much to assume, as Houssaye does, that Exelmans's first report announced that the Prussians were at Gembloux in force. This first report does not exist and can only be reconstructed, by implication, from the text of a second report, which, in my opinion, warrants no such construction.

3. There are various readings of this order, in some of which the words "or Liége" are omitted. In yet another version the sentence runs, "It is important to discover what the Prussians mean to do; either they are separating themselves from the English or intend to try their luck in another battle." I follow the text given by Houssaye which is drawn from the *Archives de la Guerre at Paris.*

at Gembloux; and it was, apparently, to meet this contingency that he had been entrusted with a force of over thirty thousand men. Further, Napoleon evidently contemplated the chance of his meeting with the entire Prussian Army, or at any rate with a superior force, otherwise he would not have added the admonition that many avenues of retreat should be kept open for the infantry.

The possibility that Wellington and Blücher might unite their armies and fight a battle to cover Brussels and Liege is treated in extremely obscure language. The only line on which a single battle could be fought to cover both places would be that of the previous day, Quatre Bras and Sombreffe, or perhaps Quatre Bras and Gembloux. Did Napoleon expect Wellington and Blücher each of them to assemble his whole army (which so far neither of them had done) and to fight another action at Quatre Bras and Gembloux, at which points the pair of them were said to be massed in strength? It must be presumed that he did, for, if the two were to fight united in a single array, they could only do so safely by converging north-west and north-east; and not a word was said to Grouchy about exploring at all in a northerly direction or west of Gembloux.

Such vagueness of instruction can only be engendered by uncertainty and confusion of thought. What Napoleon expected and hoped was that the main body of the Prussians was already withdrawing to Liege by way of Tongres and Namur, and that Grouchy would break down their rear-guard and drive it in the same direction, following it up and keeping it at a distance, while the emperor himself should fall upon the British. He gave special injunctions that frequent intelligence should be sent to him in case he should be mistaken; but he did not give Grouchy to understand that the right wing was to act as right-flank-guard to the left wing and reserve, while the emperor dealt with the British Army. It is true that a commander cannot always reveal to a subordinate all that is in his mind: that must depend on various considerations, personal and other.

If Napoleon had manifested his true meaning to Grouchy, the latter might have asked how he was to fend off ninety thousand men with thirty thousand; and the question would have been an extremely awkward one. Yet, as it seems to me, this is the gist of the whole matter, that Grouchy did not know what his master wanted, because his master either did not know or dared not tell him. The truth is that the result of the two actions on the 16th amounted to a defeat for Napoleon, and left him not indeed without resource—his genius was too

95

great for that—but with insuperable difficulties before him.

Meanwhile at nine o'clock Wellington had issued his orders for retreat. The Second British Division, part of the Fourth British Division and the Third Netherlandish Division were to march to Waterloo from Nivelles, and the Second Netherlandish Division from Quatre Bras, at once. The remainder of the Fourth Division was to halt at Braine-le-Comte. The rest of the infantry was to assemble to right and left of the position, holding its former ground only with its picquets, and at one o'clock the cavalry was to form in rear of the position in three lines to cover the march of the infantry. The corps of Prince Frederick of Orange was to retire from Enghien to Hal in the evening, and the Fourth Division (less Mitchell's brigade) was to move likewise to Hal in the morning of the 18th.

The movement, screened by all the skill of which Wellington was master, began before ten o'clock, and continued quietly, though the Duke watched the front with anxiety until the last of the battalions marched off, when he said, "Well, there is the last of the infantry gone, and I don't care now." Ney throughout this time remained perfectly inactive, which was, in the circumstances, not surprising. He had been placed in a false position on the 16th; he had suffered heavy loss for no commensurate object in consequence; he had been left all night unaware of the issue of the Battle of Ligny; and, of the letters received by him from Napoleon's headquarters on the 17th, one expressed displeasure and reproach for the isolation of d'Erlon's corps, while the other held out the prospect of a quiet day to be devoted to re-equipment and to the replenishment of stores.

To this it must be added that the discipline of the French Army was extremely bad, and that the soldiers had fallen at once into the evil ways, taught to them by many campaigns, of marauding and plunder. Even the emperor's magazines had not been spared, and the Guard had been among the worst offenders. The provost marshal, in fact, resigned his appointment on the 17th in despair over his impotence to set matters right.[4] After a hard and discouraging day's fighting in weather of intense heat, the men had probably indemnified themselves by dispersing during the night in search of such luxuries as were to be obtained by pillage; and it is reasonable to suppose that, until late in the forenoon, the ranks of many regiments were much depleted.

However that may be, there was up to one o'clock no sign of life on the French side at Quatre Bras; and Napoleon, who had arrived at

4. Houssaye, *Waterloo*.

about that hour at Marbais, losing patience made his way thither in person with Lobau's corps, the Guard, Domont's and Subervie's divisions of light cavalry and Milhaud's division of *cuirassiers*. His advanced parties struck against those of the British cavalry shortly afterwards, whereupon Napoleon deployed his force into two lines, the cavalry in front with the artillery massed in the centre, and the infantry in rear, and sent a message to Ney to advance immediately.

Wellington had for some hours past taken up his station close to Quatre Bras, sometimes seated on the ground reading and laughing over the English newspapers, sometimes riding a short distance forward to sweep the ground with his telescope. He was much astonished that the enemy made no movement, and seemed to think it within the bounds of possibility that they might have retreated. The air was intensely hot and oppressively still.

Angry thunderclouds were heaping themselves up to northward; and altogether it was such a day as saps human energy and makes even the most active man hope inwardly for peace and quiet. Wellington was undeceived by the sight of a mass of *cuirassiers* forming alongside the Namur road about two miles away—evidently the first step in Napoleon's manoeuvre of deployment.

At about two o'clock the *cuirassiers* were observed to mount and to ride forward, preceded by lancers; the advanced parties of the British horse both in the front and on the left flank became engaged; and presently a picquet of the Eighteenth Hussars came trotting in, without loss, along the Namur road. Wellington then left the conduct of the retreat to Lord Uxbridge, giving orders that anything like a serious engagement must, if possible, be avoided. Uxbridge accordingly directed the retirement to be made in three columns. The two heavy brigades of Somerset and Ponsonby, together with the Seventh Hussars and Twenty-Third Light Dragoons, formed the centre, which was to take the Brussels road; Vandeleur's and Vivian's brigades composed the left or eastern column, which was to move by Baisy and Thy; Dörnberg's brigade and the Fifteenth Hussars made up the right column, which was to pass the Thy rivulet above Genappe. Vivian's brigade, being on the extreme left, was drawn up in line at right angles to the Namur road, with its left thrown back and two guns upon the road itself.

As the French cavalry advanced, the British cannon opened fire; and then, whether owing to the concussion or not, the storm-cloud burst with a blinding flash and a terrific roar, while the rain poured down in such streams as are rarely seen even within the tropics. [5] Vivian, however, had already observed the French horse turning northward to outflank him; so, ordering his battery to retire with all speed, he put his brigade about [6] and fell back upon Vandeleur's brigade, half a mile in rear. Vandeleur, instead of waiting for Vivian's brigade to pass through his own, withdrew as Vivian approached him, wherein he was probably right, though Vivian was of a different opinion. [7] The incident showed the danger of allowing brigades to manoeuvre on their own account without the control of a divisional commander.

The French were riding fast to come up on Vivian's left and envelop him, but the ground had become so deep under the deluge of rain that their pace failed, and Vivian was able to gain the bridge over the Thy with little loss. The fire of a few dismounted men sufficed to check further pursuit by the French when they reached the bridge itself; and the brigade reached its bivouac with trifling loss.

In the centre Somerset's and Ponsonby's brigades passed through Genappe, which was the only serious defile in the road, without difficulty, and formed at the summit of a gentle slope on the north side of the village, having the Twenty-Third Light Dragoons a little in advance of them, while the Seventh Hussars as rear-guard remained on the southern side. Though the bridge at Genappe was so narrow as to admit horsemen only in single file, the Seventh was withdrawn safely across it with no great difficulty and was formed in front of the Twenty-Third, with one squadron in advance. A quarter of an hour later the French 1st Lancers debouched from Genappe, preceded by a small party of headlong troopers who proved, when captured, to be drunk.

In the narrow streets of the village the columns became so much crowded that Uxbridge ordered a squadron of the Seventh Hussars to charge. They did so, but, though received at the halt by the enemy, were unable to make any impression upon the narrow front of lances which met them in the streets. After a confused struggle of cutting and thrusting with alternations of success and failure on both sides, the Seventh were finally repulsed, and the lancers imprudently following them up the hill in pursuit were charged by two squadrons of

5. All accounts agree that the storm was of exceptional violence, and the rain extraordinarily heavy.
6. "There began at the same moment as we went threes about a shower of rain, the heaviest I ever experienced." *Memoirs of the 18th Hussars*, (I have altered the original spelling of the writer, the adjutant of the 18th, who rose from the ranks.)
7. Tomklnson, *Waterloo Letters*, by H. T. Siborne, also published by Leonaur.

the First Life Guards. Under the weight of big men on big horses the lancers were borne back in confusion into the village, where, crushed together in the narrow streets, they could not use their lances and as a natural result were very roughly handled.

The retreat was then recommenced, covered by the Union Brigade; but the pursuit was little pressed, for the ground, except on the paved road, was everywhere fetlock-deep and in the ploughed fields hock-deep, so much so that Uxbridge gradually drew the whole of his men to the road. By evening the whole had reached Wellington's chosen position on the ridge of Mont St. Jean. As usual, Wellington had hidden his troops away on the reverse slope; and Napoleon, at the head of his advanced cavalry, could see little when the head of his column came up to the ale-house called La Belle Alliance, which stands on the eastern side of the Brussels road about fourteen hundred yards south of the centre of Wellington's position.

The emperor therefore unlimbered four batteries, two of which opened fire, and deployed his *cuirassiers* as if for attack. The challenge, to Wellington's great annoyance, was at once taken up by Cleeves's and Lloyd's batteries, which opened upon the columns of French infantry whose heads had begun to show themselves about La Belle Alliance. The duke presently ordered these guns to cease fire, and Napoleon withdrew, having ascertained what he wanted to know, that the Allies were present in force.

French authors have called the retreat from Quatre Bras to Waterloo a disorderly movement, and one has gone so far as to call the French advance upon the heels of the Allies "a furious pursuit." It does indeed appear that Uxbridge, perhaps ambitious of distinction, delayed the withdrawal of the cavalry for longer than was necessary or prudent, and that for a time the retreat of a part of it was, by Uxbridge's order and example, extremely hurried. Gardiner's battery of horse artillery, according to one of its subalterns, galloped for nearly the whole of the distance, and Mercer's was also hustled backward in the same fashion. This haste seems, however, to have been urged upon the artillery only, in order to get them out of the way; and, even so, time was found to replace the cast shoe of a gun-horse of Gardiner's battery, which does not point to great pressure on the part of the pursuers.

The casualty-lists likewise fail to bear out the French contention. The total losses of the cavalry on the 17th amounted to ninety-three killed, wounded and missing, of whom forty-six belonged to the Seventh Hussars and eighteen to the Life-Guards, which were the only corps seriously engaged. The twenty-nine remaining casualties were distributed among seven different regiments, and were evidently due to the fire of artillery. A pursuit which produced no greater results could not have been very furious. Possibly, but for the heavy rain, the French might have pressed the British horse more severely; but even this is doubtful. The only time at which the French threatened any formidable enveloping movement was before the Allied rearguard had reached Genappe; and the soil was not at that period so much saturated as to impede their movements seriously. Yet they accomplished nothing; and Vivian's brigade, which was at one moment that which was in greatest danger, escaped with five casualties. Altogether Uxbridge's account of the affair is probably correct—that it was the prettiest field-day of cavalry and horse-artillery that he ever witnessed.

Throughout the afternoon and evening the rain continued with little intermission, and after nightfall it seems to have gathered new vigour and to have poured down steadily. Every soul in both armies was soaked to the skin. The tall rye, which covered most of the ground, was like standing water, and the ground was soon poached into mud knee-deep. It was difficult to light fires and impossible to keep them up. The Allies were better off than their opponents, for some at least of them had reached their bivouacs while the ground was still dry; and there was food for them when they arrived. The French infantry, on the other hand, did not come to their halting place until after dark, in some cases not until far into the night, after a most exhausting march through the mud; and the service of supply was, as usual, defective. All discipline seems to have ceased for the time.

The men dispersed in search of food and shelter, pillaging mercilessly in all directions; and many of the cavalry remounted their horses and slept all night in the saddle as the best means of keeping dry,[8] a fact which is not without its bearing on the events of the next day. Napoleon himself indicated the stations for the corps that came up with him. D'Erlon's corps and Jacquinot's cavalry were foremost about Plancenoit, about half a mile in rear of La Belle Alliance, and the cavalry of Milhaud, Domont, Subervie and of the Guard immediately to rear of them. Reille, Lobau and Kellermann's Cuirassiers stopped at Genappe. The infantry of the Guard, vainly striving to reach headquarters, for the most part lost their way and sought shelter where

---

8. If this were not narrated by a French authority (Houssaye) I should hesitate to believe it. The French had a bad reputation as horse-masters throughout the Napoleonic wars, but this is the worst example of the defect that I have encountered.

they could for the night; two or three regiments alone arriving towards midnight at Glabais, two miles south of Plancenoit. The emperor himself slept at Le Caillou, about a mile and a half south of La Belle Alliance on the Brussels road.

While the French left wing and reserve were thus engaged, Grouchy had set the right wing in march for Gembloux, bidding Gérard's corps halt while Vandamme's marched past it to take the head of the column. Vandamme moved slowly, not reaching Point du Jour, where the road from Ligny to Gembloux crosses that from Quatre Bras to Namur, until three o'clock. Arriving there at about the same time Grouchy found news from Exelmans that the Prussian army was massed on the Orneau, and that he should follow it as soon as it moved. Exelmans, however, allowed Thielmann's corps (for it was that which he had under observation) to slip away unnoticed; and, when the infantry marched into Gembloux between six and seven o'clock, much harassed by bad roads and rain, Grouchy decided to halt them there for the night.

The messages sent in by his cavalry in the evening indicated that the Prussian column, which had seemed to be marching on Namur, was really moving upon Louvain; and intelligence from peasants, confirmed by the reports of the French light horse which arrived in the course of the night, went to show that the retreating enemy was moving towards Wavre. Putting all his information together, Grouchy reported to Napoleon at ten o'clock that the Prussian Army had parted into three columns, of which one had retired on Namur, a second, which he supposed to be Blücher's, was withdrawing by the Roman road towards Liege, and a third was on its way to Wavre, presumably with the object of joining Wellington. He added that he was sending cavalry out towards the Roman road and should act according to their intelligence, following the principal mass of the Prussians in whatever direction they might take, whether to Perwez on the east or to Wavre on the north, to prevent them in this latter case from reaching Brussels and to separate them from Wellington.

But, in the orders which he issued for the morrow, he directed every part of his force to the east, evidently expecting to find the mass of the Prussians in that quarter. He seems to have regarded it as a small matter that perhaps a single corps of Blücher's army might be on its way to join Wellington. His business was to recover and to maintain contact with the main body, wherever it might be. The Prussians were assumed to have been badly beaten; and, if one column of them had turned east, towards their base, and another north, presumably (though it was by no means certain) to gain Brussels, it was most probable that the main body would wheel eastward also. So Grouchy appears to have reasoned; nor, saving the false assumption in regard to the Prussians, which was Napoleon's and not his own, did he reason unintelligently. His force was strong enough to press a defeated enemy in retreat, but not to combat an advancing enemy of thrice his strength.

Blücher, for his part, on the night of the 17th issued his orders in loyal fulfilment of his promise to Wellington. Bülow's corps was directed to march at daybreak to Chapelle St. Lambert, about four miles due east of Mont St. Jean, and Pirch I.'s to follow him to the same place. Arrived there, they were to halt and keep themselves concealed if the Allies were not seriously engaged, but, in the contrary event, they were to advance and fall upon Napoleon's right or eastern flank. Thielmann's and Ziethen's corps were to remain on the Dyle until the movements and intentions of the French at Gembloux—Grouchy's troops—should become clearer; but Blücher hoped to lead them also to the assistance of the British. This determination was taken by Blücher against the advice of Gneisenau, and, as a broad principle of action, conceded all that Wellington could have wished.

But the details of execution left much to be desired. Ziethen's corps at Bierges was within four miles of Chapelle St. Lambert as the crow flies, Thielmann's at La Bavette within five miles, Pirch I.'s at Aisemont within six miles, and Bülow's at Dion-le-Mont within seven miles. Thus, when every hour of time was precious, it was the corps remotest from Wellington which was selected to march to his aid. There was one very good reason for choosing Bülow's corps in preference to Ziethen's for this service, because Bülow's, though much harassed by long marches, had not yet been engaged, whereas Ziethen's had lost heavily both on the 15th and the 16th; but there was no such excuse to be alleged for detaining Thielmann's corps, which had not suffered severely at Ligny. Moreover, even granting that the preference of Bülow's and Pirch I.'s corps were correct, the arrangements made for their march were, to say the least, defective.

Bülow was directed not only to lead the way but to defile through the narrow streets of Wavre, whereby not merely was his journey prolonged by two miles, but the whole of Pirch's troops were compelled to mark time until the IVth Corps had passed on before them. If the Prussian staff, with Gneisenau at its head, did not foresee these complications and their inevitable result, it stands convicted of gross incompetence; if it did foresee them, and of deliberate design contrived them, it cannot be acquitted of despicable disloyalty to the Allies of Prussia and to the common cause of Europe.

Events at the Prussian headquarters in the early morning of the 18th throw further light upon the proceedings of the Staff. Pirch I.'s corps was under arms at five o'clock, but Bülow's leading division did not reach Wavre until seven. Had all gone well—and it will be seen presently that all did not go well—Bülow's corps could not have cleared the village and the passages of the Dyle before ten o'clock, so that at best Pirch I.'s corps must have lost three or four hours' rest for no object whatever. The consequences to the advance of a third corps in the same direction were still more serious. Before eight o'clock a Prussian staff-officer came in from the outposts and reported that the French at Gembloux had not moved, but appeared not to exceed fifteen thousand.

"But," he added, "if they should be thirty thousand, one corps will be sufficient to guard the line of the Dyle, for the real issue of the campaign will be decided at Mont St. Jean." Blücher, quite agreeing with this view, wrote to Müffling at half-past nine that he should lead his troops in person to attack the French right wing, as soon as Napoleon should make any movement against Wellington; and he proposed, if Napoleon should not attack on the 18th, that the British and Prussians united should attack the Emperor on the 19th. The field-marshal, beyond all dispute, was staunch enough, but not so Gneisenau. Of his own motive and without consultation with his chief, he added to this letter a postscript, begging Müffling to make quite sure that Wellington really intended to fight at Mont St. Jean, and not merely to make a demonstration, which might be fatal to the Prussian Army.

"It is of the highest importance"—such were the closing words—"to know exactly what the duke will do, in order to arrange our movements." Here we see Gneisenau naked and unashamed. Wellington had declared his intention to fight if Blücher would support him. Blücher had accepted the declaration, as made, with all possible good faith, and promised the assistance for which Wellington asked. And then Gneisenau intervened, with dark hints that Wellington designed only to entrap the Prussian Army so as to save his own, and that Blücher's promise (for such is the purport of the words quoted above) must after all depend upon fresh assurances from Müffling. No intellectual eminence can exalt a nature so essentially low as this, a nature which, from sheer terror of that which is high, abases all others to its own vile and despicable level. It was no fault of Gneisenau that the campaign of Waterloo did not end disastrously for the Allies.

While these matters were going forward, mishaps had already begun at Wavre. Bülow's leading division was hardly clear of the village when an accidental fire broke out in the principal street, preventing all passage through it; and the rest of the corps had to wait until the fire was burned out. Its march was thus delayed for two whole hours. Pirch I. was, therefore, unable to move until past noon, and at two o'clock half of his corps was still on the east bank of the Dyle. It had been decided by the Staff that, unless the French at Gembloux appeared before Wavre in too great force, Ziethen's corps and possibly Thielmann's also should follow Pirch I.; but Blücher left these details to Gneisenau, being impatient for the coming battle. He would be tied on his horse rather than miss it, he said; and at eleven o'clock the gallant old man rode off, bruised and shaken though he was, to join Bülow. But for his impetuous energy, Wellington might have fought the battle of Waterloo, for victory or defeat, without the help of a single Prussian soldier.

Meanwhile Grouchy for his part had received reports during the night which satisfied him that the bulk of the Prussians were moving north-west; and at six o'clock in the morning he sent a message to that effect to Napoleon.

> The enemy is retiring on Brussels to concentrate there or to fight a battle after uniting with Wellington. Blücher's Ist and IInd Corps seem to have gone, the one to Corbais, and other to Chaumont. I am starting for Walhain, whence I shall go to Corbais and Wavre.

There seemed to him to be no particular reason for haste, so he did not order the foremost of his infantry to march until six o'clock; and, owing to the delay in the distribution of victuals, they did not start until after seven. The whole then advanced in one column upon a single road, excepting one division which, together with three brigades of cavalry, made a bend eastward in pursuance of Grouchy's ideas of the previous night. At Walhain St. Paul Grouchy learned from a retired French officer, or from some person passing for such, that the Prussians who had marched through Wavre were on the way to the plain of La Chyse, seven miles east of the village, and were about to mass themselves there with the object either of fighting the pursuing

104

French or of joining Wellington.

He reckoned therefore that he could not do better than continue his march to Wavre, where he would be interposed between Wellington and the Prussian Army, and from whence, if the Prussians should move towards Brussels, he could reach the capital before they did. He wrote a letter to this effect to Napoleon, adding that Wellington was no doubt retreating before the Emperor; and a heavy distant cannonade which he heard in the direction of Mont St. Jean an hour or two later availed not, in spite of the remonstrances of his generals, to make him change the direction of his march. He reasoned once again from Napoleon's hypothesis that the Prussians could not have recovered from their defeat, that they had no alternative but to retire, and that, as a natural consequence, Wellington must retreat also.

Napoleon, as the originator of this delusion, of course cherished it with unshaken attachment. It is said that he went round his outposts at one o'clock in the morning to be sure that Wellington was not escaping by stealth. Soon after dawn came in Grouchy's letter, written at two o'clock of the 17th, to the effect that, if the main body of the Prussians proved to be marching on Wavre, he would follow them to head them off from Brussels and separate them from Wellington. All, therefore, seemed to be satisfactory. Orders for the disposition of the troops had already been issued on the previous day, from which it appears that Napoleon intended to move early; but the soil was so much sodden after fifteen hours of nearly continuous rain as to make the movement of artillery extremely difficult; and the attack was therefore deferred till nine o'clock.

CHAPTER 5

Waterloo: Morning

At eight o'clock, on the morning of the 18th June, 1815, the emperor breakfasted and spoke with confidence of the issue of the coming combat. Soult was not so sanguine, and repeated an opinion which he had uttered on the previous morning, that Grouchy's detachment was too strong and that part of it should be summoned to the main army. "You think Wellington a great general because he beat you," answered the emperor; "I tell you that he is a bad general and that the English troops are bad troops, and that we will make short work of them."

Reille entering shortly afterwards, Napoleon asked his opinion of the British Army. "When well posted, as Wellington knows how to post them," he answered, "I consider it invincible by a frontal attack; but it is less flexible than ours. If one cannot beat them by a direct attack, one can do so by manoeuvring." The emperor took no notice.

Jerome presently came in and reported, on the information of a waiter at the inn at Genappe, that one of Wellington's staff, when dining there on the 16th, had spoken of a projected junction between the British and the Prussians at the entrance to the forest of Soignes. "After such a battle as Ligny," answered the emperor, "the junction of the English and Prussians is impossible for another two days; besides, the Prussians have Grouchy at their heels. It is very lucky that the English are standing fast. I shall hammer them with my artillery, charge them with my cavalry to make them show themselves, and, when I am quite sure where the actual English are, I shall go straight at them with my Old Guard." [1]

In such a frame of mind it is small wonder that he was perfectly satisfied with Grouchy's report of the previous night. The emperor informed him in reply that he was about to attack the English at

1. *Vie Militaire du Général Foy.*

Waterloo, but gave him no further order than to push on to Wavre and drive the Prussians before him. Grouchy 's letter of the morning, which reached him shortly after ten o'clock, evoked from him no further instructions. The Prussians would need two days longer to recover themselves. The English were bad troops under a bad general. There was nothing more to be said.

Wellington on his side waited, apparently, until past one o'clock in the morning of the 18th before he received Blücher's letter, assuring him that at least one Prussian corps would march to his assistance in the course of the day. It is possible, indeed, that he may have received some earlier intimation which was sufficient to satisfy him; but it is very evident that he did not at that hour count upon a decisive battle. Four letters from him, dated at three o'clock in the morning, are preserved, in each of which he alludes to the possibility that his position might be turned by way of Hal, and that Brussels might thereby be uncovered; and, to meet such a contingency, he ordered Antwerp to be placed in a state of siege, recommending all refugees from Brussels to remove themselves thither.

In the circumstances, it has astonished many that he should have taken no measures against the possibility of a retreat, to which he might be compelled either by Blücher's inability to support him or by the turning movement above mentioned. As a matter of fact, a sub-altern of Vivian's brigade did receive orders on the night of the 17th to look for a road through the forest of Soignes, parallel to the main road and east of it, whereby the brigade might retire, covering the left of the army; so it is reasonable to infer that other officers received the like instruction. [2] But the absence of any general directions in the event of a retreat shows that Wellington contemplated no immediate necessity for them. In other words, he was satisfied, either by his own judgment or by direct intimation, that he could count upon Blücher's assistance, and was resolved to stand his ground until he should be manoeuvred out of it.

That he should have expected such a manoeuvre round his right flank has caused general astonishment. The explanation, however, is not difficult. He fell into Napoleon's error of overestimating the power of his own prestige. He said a few weeks later at Paris:

I think that if I had been Bonaparte I should have respected the English infantry more after what I must have heard of them in

---

2. *Waterloo Letters.*

Spain; and that I should not have taken the bull by the horns. I should have turned a flank, the right flank. I should have kept the English Army occupied by a demonstration to attack or by slight attacks, while in fact I was moving the main army by Hal on Brussels.[3]

It is objected to such a conception that it was contrary to Napoleon's whole plan of campaign, which was to separate Wellington's army from Blücher's. But this is wisdom after the event, if not indeed a begging of the whole question. We have seen from the emperor's orders to Ney on the 16th of June that he attached great importance to the capture of Brussels, not only for its moral effect but because it would sever the British from Ostend; and this idea is wholly incompatible with the separation of the armies of the Allies. If Napoleon had listened to the warnings of Soult and Reille—and the ablest [4] French historian of the campaign admits that he would have done well to consider them seriously—the vexed question would have been settled by the choice of the flank, western or eastern, by which he decided to turn Wellington's position. The only certain thing is that he could not have separated the British at once from their base and from the Prussians by one and the same manoeuvre. The truth probably is that his projects were at no time so clear and well defined as he afterwards attempted to prove them to be.

Be that as it may, the duke, holding firmly to his opinion, left Colville's division, less one brigade, and Prince Frederick's Netherlandish corps, together some fifteen to eighteen thousand men, at Hal and Tubize, nine to eleven miles west of Mont St. Jean, with orders, issued late on the 17th, to defend the position at Hal for as long as possible. In the course of the night Colville sent a staff-officer, Colonel Woodford, to Wellington for orders. Woodford arrived early in the morning of the 18th, but at a time when it was certain that a pitched battle was imminent. The duke told him that it was too late for the division at Hal to move up, but added, "Now that you are here, stay with me." Evidently Wellington felt confident of Blücher's early appearance on the field; nor was he unreasonable, for the Prussian advanced parties were actually visible at ten o'clock filing across the Lasnes less than four miles to the west.

---

3. *Journal of Colonel James Stanhope.* MS. The writer says that the statement was made at a dinner at Grassini's in Paris in answer to the question of a French gentleman, and that he heard the words himself from the duke's own mouth.
4. Houssaye.

The morning of the 18th broke dull and overcast. The thunder-clouds had not yet quite rained themselves out; and, though they were rising and the weather generally tended to improve, there were scattered showers at different points of the line throughout the day. [5] The British, roused from their cheerless bivouac, busied themselves with looking to their arms and getting rid of the useless charges loaded on the previous day, too often by firing them off. The position of Mont St. Jean, or, as we may now call it, of Waterloo, had been studied by the Royal Engineers, who had drawn up plans of it before the opening of the campaign. It consists of two nearly parallel ridges, that of Mont St. Jean on the north and that of La Belle Alliance in the south, which run east and west, and enclose between them a narrow plain. This plain is more truly a minute watershed, from which two tiny rills flow east and west, making well-defined valleys for themselves when, on reaching the hamlets of Smohain on one side and Braine l'Alleud on the other, they change their course to a northerly direction.

There rises from it, however, a secondary ridge, which runs from a point about seven hundred yards north of La Belle Alliance for about half a mile north-westward. The difference in elevation between the highest and the lowest points of the plain does not exceed sixty feet, and the gradients are nowhere so severe as to check the speed of a galloping horse either up or down. The ground was open and unfenced, and in the summer of 1815 was for the most part covered with tall waving rye. Straight through the centre of the position runs the road from Brussels to Charleroi, marked on the southern ridge by the farm of La Belle Alliance and on the northern by that of La Haye Sainte, which stand about eleven hundred yards apart. About three hundred yards north of La Haye Sainte this road crosses another, running east and west from Ohain to Braine l'Alleud, and then turns slightly westward past the farm and hamlet of Mont St. Jean to the village of Waterloo, where it enters the forest of Soignes and runs through it to Brussels.

The heights of Mont St. Jean, which had been chosen by Wellington for his battle-ground, offered advantages which were well suited to his defensive tactics. The forward or southern slope was a fairly steep glacis, and the reverse slope was easy, so that all movements in rear of the fighting line were concealed. Along the summit, in places slightly in rear of it, ran the cross-road, already mentioned,

---

5. The contradictory reports of the weather during the day from, various quarters are most easily explained in this way. Every one knows by experience how long it is before the last drop falls after a heavy thunderstorm.

from Braine l'Alleud to Ohain, screened, eastward of La Haye Sainte, on each side by thick hedges which were impenetrable by cavalry, and passing through a succession of cuttings six or seven feet deep on the way westward to Braine l'Alleud. In advance of the right centre stands the mansion of Hougoumont, which, with its grounds, covered a rectangular space some five hundred yards square, enclosed with hedges. From north to south more than half of this area was covered by a park, the western part of which was coppice and the eastern open ground.

Near the north-western angle stands the house with its chapel, its extensive outbuildings, and its large garden, walled on the south and east sides; the whole being surrounded on the north, and more extensively on the east, by a fenced orchard. In the centre of the position La Haye Sainte, a quadrangle stoutly built of stone, was shielded on the north by a terraced kitchen-garden, and on the south by a long belt of enclosed orchard which ran along the western side of the Brussels road, and flanked it for over two hundred and fifty yards. To the rear of the farm and on the eastern side of the road were a gravel-pit and a mound, shut in at the back by a hedge which adjoined the road. The road itself was blocked by one abatis at the end of the pit, and by another in line with the south wall of the farm.

On the left of the position the farms of Papelotte and La Haie, together with the hamlet of Smohain and the mansion of Frischermont, presented a third fortified post which, like Hougoumont and La Haye Sainte, thrust themselves out like bastions in advance of the main array. The general form of the position was concave, presenting to any assailant the difficult problem, of attacking a shallow re-entrant angle.

The extreme left of the line was occupied by Vivian's brigade of light cavalry, with Vandeleur's brigade immediately on its right. Then, in succession from left to right, came the Hanoverian infantry brigades of Vincke and Best, Pack's British, Bijlandt's Netherlanders, and Kempt's British, the right-hand battalion of this last leaning its right flank upon the Brussels road. Immediately on the west side of this road stood Ompteda's brigade of the German Legion, and next to them Kielmansegge's Hanoverians and Colin Halkett's British, the whole composing Charles Alten's division. On the right of Halkett, upon the hill in rear of Hougoumont, stood in succession Maitland's and Byng's brigades of Guards. [6]

---

6. Stanhope of 3/1st Guards says in his journal, "When the battle began we had two or three squares between us and the 3rd Division; before it ended, the red-coats were the nearest battalion." The detail is not very important, (continued next page),

On the right of Byng, astride the road from Nivelle to Brussels, was Mitchell's brigade, lining the road which runs westward from that road to Braine l'Alleud. On the plateau behind Mitchell was massed Clinton's division, and, in rear of Clinton again, the Brunswick contingent was held in reserve at the village of Merbe Braine. Lastly Chasse's Netherlandish Division, with sixteen guns, held Braine l'Alleud, having one brigade thrown forward in advance of the village and at right angles to the main line of battle. Wellington to the very end was nervous for his right flank.

The only infantry in second line near the centre were Kruse's three Nassau battalions in rear of Alten's division, and Lambert's British brigade, just returned from America, which did not reach the field until eleven o'clock and was then stationed at the cross-roads just in front of Mont St. Jean. The cavalry was for the most part massed in rear of the centre, the Household and Union brigades under Somerset and Ponsonby being immediately to west and east of the Brussels road, with Van Merlen's Netherlanders to the rear of Somerset, Dörnberg's and Arentschild's brigades to Somerset's right, and Trip's and de Ghigny's Netherlanders immediately behind the Household and Union brigades. Grant's brigade stood behind the Guards, with one squadron of the Fifteenth Hussars covering Mitchell's right flank.

Of the artillery six mounted batteries were with the cavalry brigades; the two Brunswick batteries were with their own contingent, and Bean's, Sinclair's and Braun's batteries were in reserve about Mont St. Jean. Ross's battery was on the high ground behind La Haye Sainte, with two guns pointing down the road; Rogers's and Cleeves's were in front of Alten's division; Kuhlmann's and Sandham's in front of the Guards; Sympher's and Bolton's in reserve with Clinton's division.

Of the advanced posts, Hougoumont was held by four light companies of the Guards, two hundred Hanoverians from Kielmansegge's brigade and one of Prince Bernhard's Nassau battalions. La Haye Sainte was entrusted to the 2nd Light Battalion of the German Legion under Major Baring; two companies of the Ninety-Fifth Rifles occupying the gravel-pit. Smohain, Papelotte, La Haie and Frischermont were occupied by the four remaining battalions of Prince Bernhard's brigade.

The total number of Wellington's army amounted to about sixty-three thousand men, [7] of which twenty-one thousand were British,

---

though it is curious: and the memory of blue coats interposed between two masses of red is likely to be correct.
7. Houssaye gives him 67,700 men and 174 guns.

BATTLE OF WATERLOO
at ¼ past 11 o'clock, a.m.

Scale _____ ¼ _____ ½ Mile.

🏰 ▦ •••• English.
🏰 ▦ ∘∘∘∘ French.

five thousand of the German Legion, nearly eleven thousand Hanoverians, fifty-five hundred Brunswickers, three thousand Nassauers and nearly seventeen thousand Netherlanders. The cannon numbered one hundred and fifty-six, seventy-eight of them British, eighteen of the German Legion and thirty-two Netherlandish. Thanks to the importunity of Sir Augustus Frazer, three out of the seven mounted batteries were furnished with nine-pounder in lieu of six-pounder guns. Whinyates's battery was provided with eight hundred rockets in addition to its field-pieces; but, in spite of Wellington's repeated representations from the Peninsula, there were no cannon on the side of the Allies that could match Napoleon's favourite twelve-pounders.

It will be observed that in this line of battle the corps, into which the army had been originally organised, were broken up, or any rate disregarded, probably with the object of depriving the Prince of Orange of the definite command of any large number of troops. The Prince had given sufficient trouble at Quatre-Bras with his mischievous interference; and the British troops would have lost much of their confidence if they had thought that they were still to be subjected to the caprice of so unskilful a commander. It will be remarked likewise that Wellington was careful to intersperse the foreign troops among the British, leaving them nowhere without red-coats close at hand; while the Netherlanders, with the exception of Bijlandt's brigade, which lay between Pack's and Kempt's, were carefully ensconced in the villages on the extreme flanks. "Form as usual" had been the duke's sole direction to his divisional generals; and accordingly they had drawn up their troops in rear of the crest of the ridge, leaving the forward slope to be disputed only by their massed light companies under a field-officer.

Bijlandt's brigade, however, not understanding the arrangement, placed itself in line with the skirmishers. No field-works were thrown up on any part of the line, though no doubt they would have been of great advantage. Wellington on the night of the 17th ordered a company of engineers to come over from Hal and fortify Braine l'Alleud; but the men lost their way in the dark and arrived too late. Any attempts to entrench the ground on the morning of the 18th were frustrated by want of tools, or in other words by bad management. Embrasures had, however, been cut in the hedges for the guns, and both Hougoumont and La Haye Sainte had been more or less prepared for defence. The main buildings and the garden wall at Hougoumont had indeed been made fairly strong, and at La Haye Sainte the walls had been loopholed; but both posts might with a little work have been made more formidable. It appears that the duke forbade any preliminary fortification lest his intentions should be thereby betrayed.

Napoleon's line of battle was as follows: On the right stood d'Erlon's corps, with its eastern flank covered by Jacquinot's cavalry division. Of the infantry Durutte's stood on the extreme right, and next to it in succession on the left the divisions of Marcognet, Donzelot and Quiot, the last named resting its left flank on the Brussels road. The artillery was posted in the intervals of brigades. West of the road Reille's three divisions occupied the first line; Bachelu's division on the right, Foy's in the centre, and Jerome's on the left, with the artillery in the front and Piré's cavalry thrown out westward to guard the left flank. In second line, behind d'Erlon was Milhaud's cavalry corps, with Domont's and Subervie's cavalry divisions massed on its left just to east of the Brussels road.

Lobau's corps was in rear of Bachelu, with its artillery on its left flank; and Kellermann's cavalry was extended in rear of Reille, l'Héritier's division on the right and Roussel d'Harbal's on the left. In the third line, and in reserve, stood the Imperial Guard, the infantry and artillery assembled close to the road, with the light cavalry on the right and the heavy cavalry on the left. The batteries of horse-artillery were attached each to its division of cavalry. In all Napoleon counted about seventy thousand [9] men, including fifty-two thousand infantry and fifteen thousand cavalry, with two hundred and sixty-six guns. He had thus a great superiority in the matter of artillery, which was even more marked in the weight of metal than in the number of guns.

The massing of troops on and about the road revealed his intention of making his principal onset, as at Ligny, upon his enemy's centre; which, indeed, he announced in his last orders, issued at about eleven o'clock. In these he said plainly that the attack would be delivered upon Mont St. Jean at the intersection of the roads by d'Erlon's corps, and that the twelve-pounder batteries of the 1st, 2nd and 6th Corps, twenty-four guns in all, would be massed together in support of it. The assault was to be opened by Quiot's division, on the left, whose left flank would be covered by a simultaneous advance of Reille's corps; and the sappers of the 1st Corps were to be ready to barricade the village of Mont St. Jean. Wellington, on the contrary, had concentrated the best of his troops, the Guards and Clinton's division, on his

8. Houssaye gives the figure at 74,000. I have reduced this, as I have Houssaye's total of Wellington's army, by 4000.

THE CHATEAU OF HOUGOMONT.

Taken chiefly from Kennedy's 'Notes on the Battle of Waterloo.'

A, Great orchard. B, Kitchen-garden. C, Small orchard. D, Hollow road. *a*, Chapel. *b*, Chateau. *c*, Farm buildings. *d*, Cowshed. *e*, Gardener's house. *f* and *g*, Barns. *h*, Small garden. *i*, Haystack. *k*, *k*, Wall loopholed by British troops.

right, leaving the defence of his centre to Ompteda's brigade of the Legion, and to Picton's division, which last had suffered very heavily at Quatre-Bras. Strangely enough, as events turned out, the battle was conducted far more according to the preconception of Wellington than of Napoleon.

The time for this attack was fixed for one o'clock in the afternoon. The emperor's original instructions had been that all troops should be in their appointed stations by nine o'clock; but this was found to be impossible. It took much time to gather in the scattered bodies that had halted between Genappe and Plancenoit during the miserable night of the 17th. Reille's corps started, according to his account, from Genappe at daybreak, but did not pass Napoleon's headquarters—a march of three miles—until nine. The Guard, according to one authority, did not break up its bivouac until ten, and Durutte reported that he did not take his place on the field until nearly noon. [10]

It was natural that the French commanders should give their drenched and exhausted men some time to clean their arms and cook their breakfasts; but it is probable, looking to the complaints of marauding made by several French officers, that it took much time, in at any rate some regiments, to assemble the soldiers together, and that it was the indiscipline of his army, countenanced through many campaigns by the practice of living on the country, which was the true cause of Napoleon's delay in opening the Battle of Waterloo. He might of course have begun the action with such troops as he had on the field, but he judged it wiser to wait until all were practically present, no doubt comforting himself, quite reasonably, with the reflection that every hour would improve the ground for the movement of his cavalry and still more of his artillery.

Having ridden down the line of his soldiers, who received him with wild enthusiasm, the emperor shortly after eleven o'clock decided to make a demonstration on the Allied flanks, perhaps with some hope of inducing Wellington to weaken his centre. Accordingly Jacquinot's cavalry made a show of turning the Allied left about Frischermont, while Reille ordered Jerome's division to advance upon the approaches to Hougoumont. Jacquinot was speedily turned back, with some slight loss, by the muskets and cannon of the Nassauers; but Jerome's column advanced steadily towards the south-western angle of the enclosure, and threw out a cloud of skirmishers to cover the opening of the attack.

9. See Houssaye.

117

GROUND-PLAN OF THE FARM OF LA HAYE SAINTE.

(Not drawn to scale.)

→ THE GREAT ROAD—CHARLEROI TO THE ALLIED POSITION. →

A, B, C, D, Dwelling-house, stables, and cow-house, of which D is the dwelling-house.

E, A barn.

F, A passage.

G, A great gate.

H, A great gate.

I, A door.

K, A great gate.

L, M, N, Doors.

O, A well, being a square building, with loopholes flanking the door and wall.

The interior measure of the yard, from the building C, D to the building E, is 40 yards, and 45 yards from the building A, B to the wall K, L.

The buildings are very strongly roofed and built. The passage F has the same roofing as the houses.

From Kennedy's ‘ Notes on the Battle of Waterloo.’

As the French masses came into sight, three British batteries from the left rear of Hougoumont opened upon them with such effect that the columns swerved off to their left. Part of Reille's cannon then came into action and were supported, pursuant to an order from Napoleon, by Kellermann's mounted batteries. The duel of artillery became hot; and Bauduin's brigade, advancing in echelon of battalions from the left, plunged down, not without heavy loss, into the hollow beneath the southern border of the coppice. Piré's cavalry covered their left flank as they moved. With Jerome and Bauduin at their head, some of the French leaped into the wood and engaged the Nassauers and Hanoverians who were holding the border.

Twice the Allied sharp-shooters drove the enemy out into the open, and Bauduin himself was killed at the very outset. But the French skirmishers, continually strengthened as their supports came up, presently established their footing within the coppice; and, though both Nassauers and Hanoverians fought stoutly as they retired from tree to tree, they were pressed back into the orchard. The French then advanced rapidly through the wood and over the park in pursuit, but were checked at the wall of the garden, which had been pierced by two tiers of loopholes and was held by a company of the Coldstream Guards. Strive as they might with the utmost gallantry to scale the wall, the French were shot down at every point by a murderous fire. Bull's howitzer battery by Wellington's orders began to throw shells into the wood with great effect. The Guards counterattacked, the Hanoverians and Nassauers seem to have rallied to their support, and the French were driven back with heavy loss upon their supports.

A fortified post, when strenuously defended, frequently assumes in the eyes of the assailants an importance out of all proportion to its true tactical value. If the centre of the Allied line were pierced, pursuant to Napoleon's design, Hougoumont would become untenable on the spot. There was no occasion, therefore, for the French to do more than occupy the wood, at once menacing the garrison of the mansion and barring the way to an offensive movement of the Allies. But Jerome, nettled at his repulse, called up Soye's brigade to renew the attack in the coppice, and directed the remains of Bauduin's to turn the buildings by the western side. The French stormed forward with the greatest gallantry, driving the Nassauers before them; but a party of the light companies of the Coldstream and Third Guards, taking shelter behind a lane and a haystack below the south-western corner of the mansion, resisted desperately.

At length, the haystack being ablaze and their retreat nearly cut off, these ran back to the gateway in the northern front of the buildings and took refuge in the courtyard, where they began hastily to barricade the gate with whatever came first to hand. A French subaltern of the 1st Light snatched an axe from one of his pioneers and, swinging it with gigantic strength, broke down the bars. A few men rushed after him into the courtyard, but, after a brief though desperate struggle, four officers and a sergeant of the Coldstream succeeded by sheer bodily strength in closing the gate; and the little band of French soldiers, with the intrepid subaltern[10] among them, was slain to a man. Others of Jerome's skirmishers swept round the north side of the buildings, and others again, extending themselves to westward, crept up unseen through the tall rye and opening fire upon Smith's British battery, which was unlimbered above them, compelled it to retire.

Four companies of the Coldstream under Colonel Woodford, however, now came up and, driving off the skirmishers first, fell next upon the flank of the 1st Light. Caught between two fires, from within the wall and without, the French gave way immediately. Some of Soye's men, attempting to debouch from the wood into the orchard, were likewise charged by the light companies of the First Guards under Lord Saltoun and hurled back in disorder. Woodford seized the moment to strengthen the garrison within the buildings; and Hougoumont was for the present safe.

By this time Napoleon's dispositions for his main attack were nearly if not quite complete; but still Jerome chose to think that his one corner of the field was the most important. He had by this time taken the keen edge off most of the seven battalions of Bauduin's brigade, which had suffered only trifling loss at Quatre-Bras, and off the one regiment of Soye's brigade which had not been severely punished in that action. But, persisting in his onslaught, he now called battalion after battalion of Foy's division into action, making use presumably of Gauthier's brigade, for Jamin's had lost over forty officers and from six to seven hundred men on the 16th. Jerome now sent his skirmishers to creep along the eastern hedge of the park, in order to turn the enclosures by the east, while the troops in the wood advanced again to a gap in the fence which separated the coppice from the orchard.

These last met and forced back Saltoun's light companies of the First Guards, which fell back slowly from tree to tree, drawing their

10. His name was Legros. Houssaye calls him lieutenant; but it appears from Martineau's list that he was only a sub-lieutenant.

assailants under the fire of the red-coats that lined the eastern wall of the garden. At the same time Wellington sent two companies of the Third Guards down the outer hedge to meet the French flanking parties upon the eastern side; and after a sharp fight the enemy was again driven back, though the British line of defence was by this time contracted to the southern hedge of the orchard and the southern wall of the garden.

Waterloo: Afternoon

It was now somewhat past one o'clock. Shortly before one, Ney, who was in charge of Napoleon's main attack, had sent a message to say that all was ready, when the emperor, who had taken his station on a high knoll in front of the farm of Rossomme, close to the Brussels road, observed a column of troops, some five or six miles to northeast, emerging from the wood of Chapelle St. Lambert. Uncertain what they might be, he sent off a detachment of cavalry to ascertain, when a Prussian hussar, captured by a French patrol about Lasnes, was brought to him. This man, who was extremely communicative, reported that the column just observed was Bülow's vanguard, and that the entire Prussian Army had been assembled on the previous night at Wavre.

The emperor, who had already written to Grouchy, ordering him to close in towards the main French Army, now added the information gained from the Prussian prisoner, with injunctions to hasten the movement and crush Bülow, while Soult appended the further explanation, "Manoeuvre so as to join our right." Napoleon then sent out Subervie's and Domont's divisions of light cavalry to observe the movements of the Prussians, occupy the passages by which they would debouch, and join hands with Grouchy's columns as soon as they should appear. Lobau's corps was likewise detached to support this cavalry in some position where it could check the advance of this new enemy. The total number of troops thus withdrawn from the field amounted to some eight thousand infantry and three thousand cavalry, with thirty-two guns.

Before the last orders had been given, the French guns opened fire to cover the great advance upon Wellington's left centre. No fewer than eighty pieces, twenty-four of them the emperor's favourite twelve-pounders, had been massed about and before La Belle Alliance, and were now raining round-shot upon the opposite slope as fast as the gunners could load them. At about half-past one d'Erlon's infantry began to move in echelon of divisions from the left, at intervals of a quarter of a mile between divisions. Quiot's led the way immediately on the east side of the Brussels road; and then followed in succession to the right the divisions of Donzelot, Marcognet and Durutte, the whole numbering some sixteen thousand men. Quiot's division was formed with its two brigades side by side, each brigade in close column of battalions. The remainder were simply massed in close column of battalions, three ranks deep; consequently, each division, being made up of eight battalions of a strength varying from four hundred and fifty to six hundred men, took the form of a dense mass with a front of one hundred and seventy to two hundred men and a depth of twenty-four men.

The inevitable result was that out of some four thousand muskets only four hundred at most were in the firing line. This was an old fault, for which the French had suffered a score of times in the Peninsula; but it was aggravated in this instance by closing up the battalions until they practically made only one body, twenty-four ranks deep, without leaving any distance between them for deployment. Indeed it is difficult to see how these divisions could have been deployed at all unless the battalions had filed to the right or left by threes, which was an extremely awkward, if not impossible, manoeuvre under a heavy fire. To whose instructions this formation was due does not appear; but Ney, who was in command of the attack, d'Erlon, who was in command of the corps, Quiot and Marcognet, the divisional leaders, had all of them served in Spain, and should have known better than to match men so clumsily arrayed against British troops in position. However, d'Erlon's corps, having been defrauded of its share of battle on the 16th, was eager for the fight, and advanced with loud shouts to the attack.

As the French columns drew near the hostile line, they threw out skirmishers; and, as Quiot's division approached La Haye Sainte, the left brigade inclined slightly to the left to attack the farm, while the right brigade continued its advance on the east side of the road. Swarming into the orchard the French engaged three companies of the 2nd Light Battalion of the Legion, which received them with a biting fire, but were borne back by sheer weight of numbers into the barn. On the western side of the orchard, however, two companies of the ist Light Battalion and one of Hanoverian rifles poured destructive

LA HAYE SAINTE

Scale.

¼ Mile.

⎯⎯⎯ French ···· Allies.

La Haye Sainte

volleys into the flank of the advancing enemy; and, Kielmansegge having detached a light battalion to the assistance of the garrison, Baring led his men to a counter-attack. But Napoleon had detached Traverses brigade of *cuirassiers* to cover the left flank of Quiot, and these, coming suddenly upon the skirmishers just as Kielmansegge's men were joining them, caused the whole to crowd together in confusion. The *cuirassiers* charged; the counter-attack in the garden, being unsupported, gave way; the French, sweeping round the buildings, mastered the garden on the north side; and the Germans took refuge where best they could, some in the main position and some in the buildings.

Ten of their officers fell in this unfortunate affair; but the men in the buildings stood firm, and not all the efforts of the French could avail to dislodge them. Farther to the east the two companies of Rifles in the gravel-pit were outflanked and forced back upon their reserves on the mound; and these in turn, sticking to their position for too long, were obliged to retreat with some precipitation across the Ohain road, where the battalion re-formed a few yards in rear of the northern hedge. Thus La Haye Sainte was totally isolated, but remained safe in the hands of its valiant garrison.

Still farther to the east, Bourgeois's brigade, struck by the fire of the Rifles from the mound and of Ross's guns in the road, had swerved to the right close to Donzelot's division, while Marcognet's division had likewise gravitated to its left towards Donzelot's, so that practically the five brigades advanced as one. Opposed to them were four battalions of Bijlandt's Netherlandish brigade (which at noon had been withdrawn in rear of the road) in first line, and the remaining battalion, flanked to its right and left by the brigades of Kempt and Pack, in second line. The Netherlanders had been much shaken, as was pardonable in raw troops, by the fire of the French artillery; and, as the masses of the French infantry drew nearer, they became more and more unsteady.

Finally, after a little wild firing they broke and ran away, in spite of all the efforts of their officers, and taking shelter on the reverse slope of the position, refused, at any rate most of them, to come forward again. [1] In their flight they carried away with them for the moment

---

1. Once again, in spite of all the pleading of Le Bas and Wommersom, the testimony of all British narrators is so strong as to the misbehaviour of Bijlandt's brigade that I cannot reject it. Moreover, it seems to be confirmed rather than refuted by the official report of Colonel van Zuylen, upon which those distinguished authors so greatly rely. The colonel ascribes the feebleness, (continued on next page),

BATTLE OF WATERLOO
at 1/4 to 2 o'clock p.m.

Scale ½ ¼   ½ Mile.

English.
French.

the gunners of Bijleveld's Netherlandish battery, who, in contrast to its comrades of the infantry, had stood to their pieces most valiantly. Thus a large gap was torn in the Allied line, but Picton, who had marked the wavering of the Belgians, deployed Kempt's brigade, which, holding its fire until Bourgeois was within close range at some points, it should seem, within twenty yards poured in a volley and then charged with the bayonet, causing the enemy to recoil with heavy loss. In this affray Picton received a bullet in the temple and fell from his horse dead.

Donzelot meanwhile pressed on to the summit of the ridge, where he halted within forty yards of the road in order to deploy, while his skirmishers pushed on through the hedges that lined it. Marcognet, thinking deployment impossible, pressed forward without attempting to change his formation; and his leading battalions bored their way through the hedges as best they could, though not without disorder. There was nothing, to all appearance, to stop this mass, some eight thousand strong, but Pack's brigade of the Royals, Forty-Second, Forty-Fourth and Ninety-Second, which, after their losses at Quatre Bras, counted between them barely fourteen hundred bayonets.

Leaving the Forty-Fourth in reserve, Pack formed the three remaining battalions four deep and advanced, apparently in echelon from the left—for the Ninety-Second was the first to come into action—to within twenty yards of the enemy, when they fired their volleys in quick succession obliquely into the front and flank of Marcognet's column.

It does not appear that the French were thereby checked, though, having sustained much loss from the Allied artillery during the advance, they may have been for the moment staggered. According to the French account, which seems the most probable, Marcognet's leading battalions returned the fire, and leaped forward with the bayonet. The British did not at once turn, apparently, and for a few moments there was a confused and deadly fight; but the odds against them were too strong—full four, indeed if Donzelot's division be reckoned, full eight to one.

The moment was most critical. Bourgeois's brigade, though shak-

of his compatriots' fire to the fact that they were formed in two ranks instead of three, which was presumably the Prince of Orange's doing. He admits that the fall of a few files produced a gap through which the French columns advanced, that the British attacked the said columns in flank, and that he himself seconded their movement with 400 men that he had rallied. If the Netherlanders had not run away, they would have been in front of the French and more than 400 strong. Nor would the 400 have needed rallying.

en, had not given way past recovery. On its left Travers's *cuirassiers* had re-formed after cutting the Hanoverian battalion to pieces, and were advancing up the hill. On its right Donzelot was deploying on the crest of the ridge, so far undefeated, and Marcognet was threatening to sweep everything before him with the bayonet. On the side of the Allies Kempt's brigade was steady and for the moment victorious. The gunners, by or without orders, were leaving their guns and hurrying to the rear; [2] and Pack's brigade, though not past rallying, was certainly not standing firm. [3] It is small wonder that Napoleon and his staff, watching the struggle from La Belle Alliance, thought that all was going well.

But before the French columns reached the summit, Uxbridge had ordered the Union Brigade farther to the left, over against the line of Donzelot's and Marcognet's attack, and had himself taken post with the Household Brigade immediately to west of the Brussels road. As Traverses *cuirassiers* came up the slope he directed the King's Dragoon Guards and First Life Guards against their front, with the Second Life Guards in echelon to their left, and held the Blues in reserve. Traverses left being somewhat in advance was first checked, but the right, pushing on, came upon the deep cutting in the Ohain road immediately to west of the cross-ways. Scrambling down one side and up the other, they were met, before they could re-form their ranks, by the remainder of the King's Dragoon Guards and First Life Guards.

Thus caught at a disadvantage, the *cuirassiers* were broken and repulsed. Some turned straight back and galloped down the hill, pursued by the two British regiments; others inclined to their right, with the Second Life Guards at their heels, plunged into the Brussels road, and galloped down it as far as the barricade before La Haye Sainte, where, being stopped, they wheeled to their left and fled through the open space between the Ohain road and the gravel-pit.

Simultaneously the Union Brigade swooped down upon the heads of the French infantry columns, the Royals on the right assailing Bourgeois's brigade, the Inniskillings falling upon Donzelot and the Greys upon Marcognet. They were barely one thousand sabres altogether, but their approach was hidden from the French by the hollows of the reverse slope of the ridge, and their onslaught was as furious as

---

2. A sergeant of Rogers's battery actually spiked one of his guns at this time. *Waterloo Letters*.

3. See *Waterloo Letters*. The only regiment mentioned as inclined to retire is the 92nd, but I do not believe that, if they had retired, the others would have stood.

it was sudden. For a moment the French masses seethed madly as the unhappy men, tightly crowded together, strove to defend themselves with musket and bayonet; and then they dissolved into a mere pack of fugitives, flying down the slope towards their own position, with the sabres of the British dragoons playing havoc among them. As it chanced, some of Traverses *cuirassiers* were driven headlong into the broken ranks of the French infantry, increasing their confusion; and the Second Life Guards joining the right of the Inniskillings, the two regiments combined in the impartial chase of horse and foot.

Seldom in all military history has there been seen a more terrific smashing of formed infantry by cavalry. It is small wonder that the British troopers became drunk and maddened by their success. Their horses were good and fairly fresh, for there had been no weight crushing down their backs all night, as in the case of the French; the ground was in their favour; the men could not only sit in the saddle but could ride; and from ten to fifteen thousand French were retreating or flying before them. Quiot's troops, left in isolation at La Haye Sainte, abandoned the attack. Durutte on the extreme east, after driving the Nassauers from Papelotte and nearly reaching the crest of the ridge, found his right flank assailed by the Twelfth Light Dragoons, who drove him back in great confusion upon his reserves. It seemed as if the British cavalry would sweep all before them; and no sound of voice or trumpet could make the men stop.

The Household and Union Brigades galloped on over the plain and up the acclivity of La Belle Alliance, until the former came under the fire of Bachelu's division, which had been slightly advanced to cover d'Erlon's flank during his attack, and were received with a storm of bullets which overthrew many men and scores of horses. Then, seeing a compact body of *cuirassiers* advancing against them, they wheeled about and retreated, the Blues, which were less out of hand than the rest, striving to cover the retreat. Farther to the left the Greys, with some of the Royals and Inniskillings, dashed into the midst of two divisional batteries, halfway up the ridge, cut down gunners, drivers and horses, upset the guns into a ravine, and then swinging sharply to their left assailed Napoleon's great battery of eighty pieces. The emperor ordered two regiments of Delort's *cuirassiers* to attack them; but, before these could move, the 3rd and 4th Lancers of Jacquinot's division fell upon the left flank of the British and bade fair to annihilate them. In no kind of order, and with horses blown and exhausted, the remnants of the Union Brigade could make little resistance nor even attempt to fly.

Sir William Ponsonby was borne down and killed, and indeed few of them would have escaped, had not the Twelfth and Sixteenth Light Dragoons of Vandeleur's brigade come to their rescue, charged the French lancers in turn, and given their comrades some respite. Thus tardily and with difficulty the remnants of the two brigades crawled back to their places behind La Haye Sainte. Of two thousand troopers and horses that had charged, over one thousand horses and from seven to eight hundred men were killed, wounded and missing. The Twelfth Light Dragoons also had lost their Colonel, Frederick Ponsonby, who was desperately wounded, and the strength of a whole squadron either hurt or slain.

Over the greater part of the field there was now a lull, except for a continuous duel of artillery, while both sides regained their positions. D'Erlon's losses had been very heavy; and both Bourgeois's brigade and Marcognet's division were for the present unfit for further action. At least two thousand French prisoners had been captured. In one place their muskets lay in rows on the field as if they had been grounded by word of command; and the panic was so great that some of the fugitives ran as far as Genappe before they could be stopped. [4]

Twenty or thirty French guns had been disabled. The eagles of the 105th and 45th were taken; and the moral effect of the charge of the Union Brigade was strong and permanent. On the other hand, Donzelot's division, though not unscathed, had retired in comparatively good order, and the Allies had paid a heavy price for their success. The two finest brigades of the British cavalry had almost ceased to exist; and there was a strong feeling that, if they had been supported, their success might have been more far-reaching and more permanent. Uxbridge, in fact, had been unable to resist the temptation of leading the first line of the Household Brigade himself; the Blues and the Greys, which he had designed to act as reserves, had both been drawn into the main attack; and at the critical moment there was no general director of the whole movement and consequently no support at hand to maintain the leading squadrons. Uxbridge reproached himself bitterly to the end of his days for his fault; but the mischief was done and could not be amended.

Moreover, one Hanoverian battalion had been annihilated. Bijlandt's brigade, though the officers had wrought their utmost to hearten the men, was to all intent out of action; and hundreds of

4. Houssaye.

the Netherlandish soldiers were hidden away in the forest of Soignes, where they lay at their ease with piled arms, cooking their soup and smoking until the time should come for them to advance in safety or to disperse to their homes, as the fortune of the day might dictate.

Round Hougoumont the struggle never ceased to rage with extreme bitterness, as Foy and Jerome threw more and more of their battalions into the fight. Byng was obliged to relieve Saltoun by sending down his battalion of the Third Guards, which cleared the orchard by a counter-attack and, establishing itself along the southern hedge, restored security. Napoleon then sent a battery of howitzers to play upon the buildings, and, the shells setting fire to a barn, the flames rapidly spread to the mansion, stables and cowhouses. The garrison, reinforced by a battalion of Brunswickers and another of Duplat's brigade, none the less continued their resistance.

The wounded lying in the burning buildings were left perforce to their fate in spite of many efforts to rescue them; but the survivors fought on. The fire fortunately stopped at the chapel; the French infantry, disheartened by many failures, no longer showed the same resolution in attack; and, ensconced in the chapel and in such other out buildings as had escaped destruction, the defenders held grimly on to Hougoumont.

Waterloo: Late Afternoon

It was now about three o'clock. Wellington had brought Pack's brigade forward to take the place of Bijlandt's, summoned Lambert's brigade to the support of the Fifth Division, and closed in the whole of his left towards the centre. The Rifles also had reoccupied the mound at La Haye Sainte; and two fresh companies had been sent into the buildings, the defence of the orchard being now abandoned. The emperor now reinforced Reille's artillery by some of the Guards' twelve-pounders, making them up to thirty-four pieces, and ordered them, together with the grand battery, to play upon the right and left centre of the Allies. The cannonade was more intense than the oldest soldier among the Allies had ever experienced, and Wellington withdrew the first line along a great part of his left centre a hundred yards farther to the rear, so as to give them better shelter.

Under cover of this shower of shot and shell Ney led Quiot's troops once more to the assault of La Haye Sainte, while one of Donzelot's brigades advanced, not in columns but in loose swarms, to cover his right flank. Once again the main attack failed before the steadfast defence of the German Legionaries under Baring; and Donzelot's skirmishers, meeting Kempt's and Lambert's brigades halfway up the hill, were driven back before they could make any headway. In fact, the onset appears to have been half-hearted, perhaps because the French had not yet recovered from the shock of their previous repulse; and in many narratives of the battle it is not even mentioned. [1]

The general retrograde movement of the Allied infantry upon the reopening of the cannonade had, however, caught the eye of Ney, who, misconstruing it as the beginning of a general retreat, conceived the

---

1. See Houssaye. The authorities quoted by him establish beyond doubt the fact that this second attack was delivered.

idea of establishing a footing on the plateau with cavalry. He therefore summoned Farine's brigade of Delort's division of *cuirassiers*; and, when Delort pleaded that he could take no orders except from Milhaud, who commanded the corps, the marshal, much incensed, directed not only the brigade but the entire corps to advance with him. Lefebvre-Desnoëttes's light cavalry of the Guard followed likewise, with or without orders; and eight regiments of *cuirassiers*, one of lancers and one of mounted *chasseurs*, five thousand men in all, trotted down to the low ground just to west of the Brussels road to form for the attack.

Wellington and his staff stood amazed. He had looked, possibly, for a still more formidable assault upon Hougoumont; and, as most of Byng's brigade had already been swallowed up by the first attack, he had brought forward four Brunswick battalions from Merbe Braine to fill the vacant place. But a charge of cavalry upon unbroken infantry seemed, after the experience of Quatre Bras, sheer madness. The infantry, drawn up by battalions chequerwise, received orders to form square, and the gunners were bidden to fire to the very last moment, and then to take shelter in the nearest squares, removing first the near wheel from every gun and trundling it before them to their refuge. [2]

Just before Ney set his cavalry in motion, Piré's horse made a demonstration with both squadrons and battery against the British right, drawing off the Thirteenth Light Dragoons and Fifteenth Hussars of Grant's brigade, as well as the Second Light Dragoons of the Legion, to oppose it. The trumpets then rang out, and the noble array of horsemen began to move, *cuirassiers* on the right, *chasseurs* and lancers on the left, in a north-westerly direction obliquely across the valley, so as to strike the Ohain road where it ran level with the rest of the ground. Their formation was in echelon of columns of squadrons,[3] with the right, presumably, leading; and since their front, straitened as it was between Hougoumont and La Haye Sainte, can little have exceeded eight hundred yards, they must have presented an ideal target for artillery.

Their advance cannot have been rapid, for the rye rose well above their girths, [4] and the ground beneath it, being still wet, must soon

---

2. This last detail is chronicled in the *Life of Sir William Gomm*; but is probably best known to the mid-Victorian generation through the pages of Henry Kingsley's *Ravenshoe*.

3. Houssaye.

4. I never realised how immensely heavy were the rye-crops on the field of Waterloo until I found in the Royal Collection at Windsor Castle nine water-colour drawings of the field, made by Denis Dighton on the days immediately following the battle—in fact, before the dead had been buried.

HOUGOMONT

Scale of ¼ Mile.

English
French

GRANT

TO Comte

M. HALKETT

M. HALKETT

DU PLAT

BRUNSWICK

BRUNSWICK

from Braine l'Alleud

Hougomont

PRINCE JÉROME

PIRÉ

to Rossomme

FOY

FOY

RICHÉ

ROUSSEL

to Belle Alliance

to

have been poached into deep mud. The pace too must have decreased as they breasted the hill, which no doubt soon became slippery, and such horses as had been loaded with their riders all night must speedily have flagged. The French artillery necessarily ceased firing as they ascended the ridge; and the French cavalry's line being oblique to that of the Allies, Wellington's guns were able to pour a tempest of shot not only into their front but into their flanks, blasting away whole heads of squadrons when they came within close range. The French horsemen naturally wavered, for they could hardly move forward over the heaps of dead horses.

Indeed, opposite Mercer's battery, not far from the north-eastern corner of the orchard of Hougoumont, the front ranks turned and, finding themselves pressed forward by the rear ranks, actually fought them with blows and curses in their eagerness to ride back; while Mercer's nine-pounders, doubly loaded with case and round-shot, riddled the seething masses from end to end.

Elsewhere the French cavalry rode into the batteries, but found themselves none the better for it. They could not carry off the guns, and they possessed no means of spiking them. They could only pass through the intervals with ranks thinned and disordered, spur their horses into some semblance of a gallop and fall upon the squares. But, the farther they went, the more their front was contracted between the cuttings of the Nivelles road and the Brussels road, so that the squadrons became crowded together and their pace was checked.

Moreover, the squares being arranged chequerwise, it was impossible to assail any one of them except under a flanking fire from others. Here, therefore, as at Quatre Bras, the French cavalry was reduced to an aimless wandering in and out of the squares, suffering very heavy loss and inflicting very little damage. Uxbridge meanwhile collected six regiments from the Brunswick cavalry, Grant's, Dörnberg's and Arentschild's brigades, with which, backed by three brigades of Netherlandish cavalry, he made a counter-attack, which swept the cuirassiers clean off the plateau into the dead ground under the southern slope of the ridge.

The Allied gunners instantly ran back to their guns and replaced the wheels; and meanwhile Wellington, ceasing to be anxious for his right, had considerably altered his dispositions in that quarter. Clinton's division was moved up from its place in reserve into the front line. Hew Halkett's Hanoverian brigade was placed as a support to the Brunswickers on Maitland's right; the Twenty-Third from Mitchell's brigade was posted in the middle of the Brunswickers to give them the countenance of a veteran regiment; Adam's brigade was stationed on their right; and Duplat's brigade took up its position on the slope in rear of Hougoumont to be ready to reinforce that post.

These changes appear to have been completed when the French cavalry, having rallied with amazing quickness, appeared once again upon the comb of the ridge and renewed their attack. For the second time they trotted through an appalling fire of artillery into the deserted batteries and passed on to repeat their futile gyrations round and round the squares. Unable to pierce the hedges of bayonets, small parties of brave men engaged the red-coated infantry with their pistols, hoping to provoke the face of some square to waste a volley upon them and so to give a reserve, which was kept in rear of them, the chance of charging an array of empty muskets. Their efforts were fruitless. Not a red-coat fired except by word of command.

The horses, by this time unable to trot, walked round and round the bayonets in helpless swarms till they were shot down; and the second attack failed as completely as the first. The French cavalry, therefore, fell back down the hill; and as they went, two columns of Quiot's and Donzelot's infantry, which had advanced against La Haye Sainte, fell back likewise; while some battalions of Foy's division, which had crept up into the orchard of Hougoumont to turn the flank of the garrison, were driven back into the coppice by the Third Guards.

From the heights of La Belle Alliance the appearance of the opposite plateau, with the French horsemen swarming through the batteries and about the squares, apparently masters of the ground, made many of the French think that the victory was won. Napoleon himself may have thought so for a moment, but he was soon undeceived; and Soult, who knew the ways of Wellington, was probably not deluded for an instant. The emperor realised that Ney's attack had been premature, but, being committed to it, he decided to support it, and sent orders to Kellermann and Guyot to lead their ten regiments to the charge. Kellermann was inclined to demur; but l'Héritier marched off his division at the trot without awaiting further orders, and Kellermann had no option but to follow with the other.

Napoleon, in his own narrative, declared that he wished to hold Guyot's brigade of the Guard in reserve, and tried to recall it; but it seems certain that he did nothing of the kind. Beyond doubt he hoped to gallop over the right centre of the Allies and finish off the battle without further ado; and he hoped so, because he was beginning to realise that, unless he could do so, he might sustain a disastrous defeat.

Blücher had overtaken Bülow's corps at Chapelle St. Lambert at about one o'clock and had at once sent out patrols to explore the passages of the Lasnes and of Paris Wood, which covered the ground for some fifteen hundred yards, north and south, beyond it. At about two o'clock, when Bülow's rear-guard was yet an hour's march away, the patrols returned with the report that the French were still at a safe distance; and the field-marshal at once gave the order to march upon Plancenoit. The roads were infamous, the descent to the Lasnes being very steep and the ascent from the stream westward even steeper; and the men were weary after an exceedingly trying march, and weak from long fasting. It seemed hopeless to attempt to drag guns axle-deep in mud up so heavy an incline; but Blücher would hear of no difficulties. Along the line of march he was cheering and encouraging his men. "I have promised Wellington," he kept saying to them. "You would not have me break my word."

His strong will and fiery energy stimulated even the most sluggish to extreme effort; and at about four o'clock the heads of his columns reached the western border of Paris Wood, where the two leading divisions halted in concealment. Blücher would gladly have waited for the rest of Bülow's corps to come up; but Wellington's messages, bidding him hasten, became more and more urgent; and at half-past four the two divisions, covered by two regiments of cavalry and three light batteries, emerged from the wood right and left of the Plancenoit road. His guns unlimbered and opened fire upon Domont's squadrons, which, after a dash upon the Prussian hussars, fell back slowly, and then wheeling off right and left revealed Lobau's corps extended in two lines astride the road, about a mile and a half east of the highway to Brussels. Lobau, promptly taking the offensive, drove the Prussians back; and Blücher was fain to halt until the rear of Bülow's column should close up.

The Prussians Arrive

Blücher's guns must have been heard both by Wellington and Napoleon soon after half-past four. His first engagement with Lobau must have occurred between five and half-past five, just as Kellermann's and Guyot's squadrons were forming in the low ground, with the wreck of Milhaud's corps streaming back all round them. Milhaud's men quickly rallied behind the new array; and the whole moved forward once again, sixty squadrons some nine thousand strong, all cramped within a front which could barely have held nine hundred horsemen, knee to knee, without any intervals whatever. The French batteries, as before, preluded the attack by a terrific cannonade, which was continued to the last moment and ceased only as Kellermann's squadrons breasted the ascent.

Advancing on the track of their predecessors, they could not move fast over ground poached deep by the trampling of thousands of hoofs, and fared no better than they. The front ranks were torn to tatters by the Allied artillery as they ascended the slope to the batteries, and, when the survivors had passed by the abandoned guns, they were sucked by a dozen channels into the intervals between the squares, where they eddied round and round them in streams and backwaters, now firing their pistols, now charging resolutely in small bodies, but always beaten off by the steady fire from behind the bayonets. There were squares that sustained many attacks, but it does not appear that one of them was broken. [1] There was no particular reason why they

1. The French (see Houssaye) claim to have broken two or three squares and to have taken two colours, one from a British battalion and one from a battalion of the German Legion. British and Legion, as is well known, have never admitted that a square was broken, much less that a colour was lost, at Waterloo. Vague claims to the capture of colours are too common in the

should have been, for there was no thunder of hoofs growing momentarily louder, no wall of dust rushing steadily nearer, no awful emergence of maddened horses and gleaming blades in endless lines and waves from the dust-cloud, no element, in fact, of the terror which cavalry can strike into infantry even in the manoeuvres of peace.

Instead of all this there were simply swarms of exasperated men on weary horses, who walked round and round, fetlock-deep in mire, swearing loudly and making desperate thrusts from time to time through the hedge of bayonets, but doing very little harm and offering generally a capital target. The incessant procession of these walking cavaliers might have terrified young soldiers for a moment, but old soldiers never. Whether to young or to old it was an ordeal incomparably less trying than to lie down, either in line four deep or in square, amid the bursting shells and wicked ricocheting round-shot which earlier in the day had poured in an unbroken stream from the French batteries. Under such a fire men could only endure and hope, for there was no means of reply; but, within squares safely closed up, the disjointed attacks of walking *cuirassiers* were not very dangerous, and afforded endless opportunities for telling return blows.

Gradually the French horsemen began to retire down the slope, first in small parties, then in broken squadrons, and finally in complete masses. The British gunners rushed back to their cannon, but had barely time to fire a few rounds into the backs of their enemies before a fresh array came up the hill with its left close to the eastern fence of Hougoumont, This was Blancard's brigade of *carabineers* which Kellermann, with excellent judgment, had hidden in a fold of the ground during his advance, to act as a reserve. These now advanced up the height, backed, apparently, by a brigade of *cuirassiers*; but at this moment Grant, having undeceived himself as to the true intent of Piré's demonstration on Wellington's extreme right, had left one squadron

reports of French officers during the Peninsular War to carry the slightest weight with me. The receipt of a captured British colour signed by Grouchy's *aide-de-camp* (quoted by Houssaye) is something more definite, but would deserve greater credit if it stated the regiment to which the colour belonged. I have never heard of a colour lost at Waterloo; and, as the loss of its colour by the 69th at Quatre Bras was not concealed, I do not see how such a mishap could have been kept secret by any regiment. The 9th Cuirassiers, who claim to have taken a colour at Waterloo, were engaged at Quatre Bras and may have been the captors of the 69th's colour, which may have been handed over to Grouchy as having been taken at Waterloo. The 9th lost two officers at Quatre Bras and thirteen at Waterloo: and in the general disorganisation after the latter's action the mistake could easily have been made.

of the Fifteenth to watch the French horse in that quarter, and returned to his original place in rear of Hougoumont.

Forming the Thirteenth Light Dragoons in line he launched them at the flank of the *carabineers*, and a few minutes later directed the Fifteenth Hussars upon the flank of the *cuirassiers*. Both charges were successful, driving the enemy down the hill upon their main body. This last, however, having rallied, now with the greatest gallantry renewed its attack; and the Thirteenth and Fifteenth were compelled to fall back, which they did with great steadiness, to the rear of the infantry.

Once again the tide of the French cavalry surged into the intervals between the squares, flooding the space up to the bayonets but there stopping and rippling round them through channels now cumbered with the corpses of man and beast, powerless to break over the immovable boulders of red-coats. No men could have showed more persistent bravery than the French troopers; but they were opposed to adversaries as stubborn as themselves. After a time, as the more daring spirits were struck down, the attack became feebler and feebler. Riders and horses were in fact exhausted. The atmosphere was still heavy and thunderous, and the crowding of a vast mass of men and horses, all alike heated by extreme exertion, made the temperature almost insupportable.

A stream of dismounted cavaliers was constantly pouring to the rear; small parties began to follow them; the whole wavered irresolutely, then, upon the advance of the Allied cavalry, gave way and were swept over the plateau. Their losses had been frightful. Ney, having had three horses killed under him, was afoot, raging with fury. In Kellermann's corps both divisional generals and three brigadiers were wounded and the fourth brigadier was killed. In Milhaud's corps both divisional generals and three out of four brigadiers were wounded, and in the cavalry of the Guard General Guyot was wounded. Hardly a general officer was left standing, and there was not a regiment of *cuirassiers* which had lost less than a dozen officers. Nevertheless it seems that Ney gathered the wreck of them together for a fourth charge, which was as gallantly delivered as the condition of the horses would permit, but failed as completely as all the rest. The flower of the French cavalry had been wrecked upon a score of attenuated squares.

Ney now resorted to the tactics which he should have employed at first; namely, to use infantry and cavalry in conjunction with each other. Wellington, anticipating some such design, had some time before ordered Chassé's Netherlandish Division to march to a hollow in rear of the Guards so as to liberate Duplat's and Adam's brigades for work in the front line, and had reinforced his artillery by two batteries. In due time two columns of Bachelu's and Foy's divisions, supported by cavalry, advanced against the centre of the Allied right wing under a heavy fire from the British guns. "*It was a hail of death*," wrote Foy afterwards; and the French infantry quailed under it. Bachelu's men turned first and carried away Foy's in their flight. Foy himself was wounded, but rallied his men in the ravine to the south of Hougoumont before he left the field. The attack was then renewed and was met and checked for a time by a charge of Somerset's Household Brigade.

But Trip's Netherlandish cavalry, which were in support, refused to move forward; and, when they saw the *cuirassiers* moving forward against them, they turned and galloped to the rear, greatly disordering the 3rd Hussars of the Legion in their flight. The 3rd, presently rallying, charged and broke the *cuirassiers* immediately opposed to them, but were enveloped by others upon their flanks and were fain to retreat to the rear of the squares with very heavy loss. Uxbridge then called upon another Netherlandish regiment, the Cumberland Hussars, to move forward; but in this corps the rawness of the men was supplemented by the cowardice of their colonel; and, in spite of all efforts to make them stand, even out of fire, these wretched creatures galloped off to Brussels, spreading panic as they went.

Meanwhile, Wellington had ordered Duplat's brigade to reinforce the right centre; and the rifle-fire of its four light companies compelled the line of French horse to withdraw. The remainder of the brigade then came up, together with Sympher's battery, and formed squares to resist the second line of French horse; but the French skirmishers during the attacks of the cavalry had seized the opportunity to creep up under the eastern hedge of Hougoumont to the brow of the main position, from whence they poured in a most galling fire upon the squares. Duplat fell mortally wounded, and the horses of all the mounted officers were killed; but it was impossible for the Germans to deploy, from fear of a charge from the enemy's cavalry. The charge was presently delivered, and was manfully beaten off; whereupon the skirmishers swarmed forward again to ply the squares with bullets while the French mounted batteries unlimbered to scourge them with grape, so as to prepare the way for another charge.

Through this most trying ordeal the bearing of Duplat's battalions was wholly admirable; and presently they were relieved by the advance of Adam's brigade, in two lines four deep, with Wellington himself at their head. The moment was most critical, for the gunners of the Allies had been driven from their guns, and the French skirmishers in great force had opened a very heavy fire upon Adam's advancing battalions. "Drive those fellows away," ordered the duke calmly; and the Seventy-First together with the eight companies of the Rifles [2] obediently drove them from the crest, halted in a slight hollow near the north-east angle of the Hougoumont enclosures and formed squares, the Seventy-First on the right, the Fifty-Second in squares of wings in the centre, and the Ninety-Fifth on the left. They were promptly assailed by Guyot's brigade of the Imperial Guard, but they received them with volleys so telling that after several charges the French drew off, there being few but dismounted men left to retire. Two battalions of Hew Halkett's Hanoverian brigade then advanced to the southern slope of the ridge, taking post to the rear of Duplat; and the right centre of the Allies was thus firmly re-established.

Simultaneously Ney had directed a part of Donzelot's division upon La Haye Sainte. Baring, who was short of rifle-ammunition, sent urgent messages for a supply but could obtain none, though three additional companies were sent to reinforce his garrison. The French made a desperate attempt to break in by an unclosed doorway, opening on the south side into a barn, and, failing, set the barn itself on fire. With great readiness Baring ordered his men to fill their camp-kettles at a pond in the yard, and though many lost their lives in thus fetching water, he succeeded in extinguishing the flames. While these were thus desperately engaged with one party of the enemy, another swarm of French skirmishers advanced beyond the buildings on the western side, with the intention either of breaking in on the north side or of cutting of the post altogether from the main position.

There upon the Prince of Orange ordered the 5th and 8th battalions of the Legion to deploy and advance; and the brave Germans, hoping that there would now be an end of lying down under a heavy cannonade, ran eagerly forward driving the French before them. The 8th, which was in advance, was on the point of charging with the bayonet when a body of French cuirassiers, fresh from an unsuccessful attempt upon Kielmansegge's squares, suddenly burst upon their right flank by surprise and rolled them up from end to end. The unfortunate battalion was practically annihilated, most of its officers were killed, and the king's colour was captured. None the less the attack

2. 2nd batt.: 6 cos.; 3rd batt.: 2 cos.

on La Haye Sainte was beaten off, and Baring with his noble garrison remained still in proud possession.

It was now not far from six o'clock, and in due course of time two more of Bülow's divisions had debouched from Paris Wood. Blücher resumed his advance against Lobau, but was met with so stout a resistance that he was fain to abandon his frontal attack and gain ground by manoeuvring to turn his opponent's right flank. Lobau thereupon fell back to the level of Plancenoit, throwing one brigade into the village. Blücher then assaulted Plancenoit from three different points, drove out the French garrison, entrenched himself there, and bringing forward his artillery opened a cannonade, throwing some shot as far as the Brussels road. Twice during the course of these operations urgent messages came in from Thielmann at Wavre, saying that he was attacked by superior numbers and doubted his power to hold out against them. But Gneisenau had a great as well as a small side, and on this day the greatness was uppermost. "Let Thielmann defend himself as best he may," he answered; "it is no matter if he be crushed, so long as we gain the victory here."

With a new enemy pressing upon his right flank and arrived within cannon-shot of his main line of communications, Napoleon realised that no time must be lost. He gave orders to Duhesme's division of the Young Guard to retake Plancenoit, and directed Ney to master La Haye Sainte at any cost. Durutte he had already instructed to make a fresh attack upon Smohain, so as to take pressure off Lobau. Duhesme's eight battalions did their work nobly, driving the Prussians from Plancenoit with irresistible dash. Ney, hurrying to the head of the 13th Light, led them against La Haye Sainte; and Baring called upon his men for yet another effort. It was a hard moment for him. The stock of ammunition was reduced to two or three rounds a man, and for some reason rifle-cartridges, though frequently and pressingly sought, were still not forthcoming.

Not the less did his men promise cheerfully to stand by him to the last; and this new onset of the French was met with the same gallantry as the first. Once again the barn was set on fire and once again the flames were extinguished; but, as rifle after rifle fell silent for want of ammunition, the French gained ground. Baring, slowly retiring to the garden, made his men return singly to the main position, where they rejoined their regiments; while he himself joined two companies of the 1st Light battalions close to the cross-roads. No men could have borne themselves more heroically than these defenders of La Haye

Sainte; but there was no disguising the fact that, though it was no fault of theirs, the key of Wellington's centre was lost.

Realising his advantage Ney begged the emperor for fresh infantry to turn it to account. "Where am I to get them?" answered Napoleon testily. Do you expect me to make them?" [3] There was nothing for it but to assemble the shattered remains of Donzelot's and Quiot's divisions, with the remains of the cuirassiers, to support the attack on the centre, while the remnants of Reille's corps were set in motion for a supreme attempt against Hougoumont. The actual victors of La Haye Sainte were able from the garden and buildings to command the knoll by the sand-pit with their fire, and to drive away the two companies of Riflemen which held it; and then, bringing up two guns to the bank of the high road, they poured a storm of grape upon Kempt's brigade on the other side of it.

The Riflemen speedily put a stop to this by picking off the gunners; but fresh guns were brought up to a spur over against the middle of the British right centre, which played havoc with the Allied batteries. Now a fresh column of French issued from behind the farm and, extending into a close line of skirmishers, fell upon Ompteda's devoted brigade of the Legion. Alten sent orders to Ompteda to deploy, if practicable, and drive these tormentors off. Ompteda, knowing that *cuirassiers* were lying in wait in rear of the sharp-shooters, deprecated any such measure; but at this moment the Prince of Orange rode up and, deaf to all protestations, peremptorily ordered Ompteda to deploy. Ompteda could only obey, and placing himself at the head of the 5th battalion led it forward to the charge. The French fell back to La Haye Sainte, where they took shelter among the enclosures; and then, as Ompteda had predicted, a regiment of *cuirassiers* fell suddenly upon his right flank and swept his men out of existence.

The Riflemen on the other side of the road, after long hesitation from fear of hitting friends as well as foes, now poured in a volley which staggered the cuirassiers; and the 3rd Hussars of the Legion galloping forward cleared the whole front of Ompteda's brigade until compelled by the arrival of fresh bodies of French horse to retire. In this affray Ompteda, a most gallant officer, was killed, an immolation to the ignorance and self-sufficiency of the Prince of Orange. The prince himself was presently forced by a wound to quit the field, and none too soon. In two days he had succeeded in destroying three good

---

3. Everyone assigns a different time to this celebrated speech: but this seems to me the most likely moment.

battalions of the British and German infantry, each one by the repetition of the same foolish mistake.

Another body of French skirmishers now turned north-west from La Haye Sainte, threatening alike Maitland's brigade, of which the Third battalion of the First Guards, formed in square, was posted in advance of the rest, and the square of Riflemen which formed the left of Adam's brigade. Both were suffering severely when Wellington ordered the Guards to deploy and charge, which they did, re-forming square instantly as the French cavalry came up. The latter shrank from the attack, but too late to escape from the bullets of the Guards; and then, losing their heads, they galloped along the whole front of the Fifty-second, losing scores of men from the fire of that regiment. The pressure upon the Guards was thus relieved; but immediately afterwards the principal onslaught upon Hougoumont was developed by Reille's corps.

The mansion was by this time nearly burned out, but the outhouses, except on the south side, were still aflame; and the defenders were much harassed by the heat and smoke. Nevertheless their resistance was as strenuous as ever. The flank-companies of the Guards still held the walls and buildings. The Coldstream lined the hedge that bordered the main approach to the mansion. The Third Guards occupied the orchard, and, though driven back at first to the road beyond it, recovered themselves with the help of the light companies and the 2nd German battalion of Duplat's brigade, finally, after many vicissitudes of fortune, re-establishing their position at the front hedge of the orchard.

All therefore was well with Hougoumont; but all was not well in the centre. From the knoll above the sand-pit—their other point of vantage—the French skirmishers poured an active and deadly fire upon the troops right and left of the Brussels road. Kempt's and Lambert's brigades, though sorely tried, replied with spirit enough, though the Twenty-Seventh, lying in square in the north-eastern angle of the cross-roads, suffered terribly. But the survivors of Ompteda's brigade were beginning to steal to the rear, and it was evident that they were exhausted as a fighting force. He would be a stern judge that would blame them, for two out of the four battalions had been cut to pieces and the other two cruelly punished.

Kielmansegge's young battalions also were much shaken. Alten, Colin Halkett and Ompteda had fallen; and Kielmansegge, who was striving desperately to rally his own men, was left in charge of the division. A dangerous gap was, in fact, opened and slowly widening in the British centre, and the situation was critical in the extreme. Somerset, with the wreck of his brigade extended in rank entire, so as to make a show, was endeavouring to instil confidence into the Hanoverians and to keep them in their places. He had been ordered some time before to withdraw and to take shelter from cannon-fire, but had answered that the slightest movement would make the Netherlandish cavalry, which were in support of him, turn and run.

The situation was happily saved by Vivian, who, without orders, brought up his brigade of light dragoons and, forming them in rear of the wavering battalions, brought them to a stand; and Wellington presently brought up five Brunswick battalions from the second line to fill the gap more thoroughly. These last were not at first very steady; in fact they gave way in a body. They were not without excuse, for they were very young soldiers and they had been led straight into the post of greatest danger; but through the efforts of Wellington and other officers they were rallied. Vandeleur's brigade was presently sent up by Uxbridge to join Vivian; and a very dangerous crisis was successfully passed.

It was now seven o'clock; and meanwhile Blücher had not been idle. Rallying the repulsed battalions of Bülow's corps, he made a strong counter-attack upon Plancenoit, drove the Young Guard from it, and, again bringing forward his artillery, began to throw shot dangerously near to La Belle Alliance itself. Napoleon thereupon formed eleven battalions of the Guard in squares along the road from Rossomme to La Belle Alliance, and sent down two battalions of the Old Guard to retake Plancenoit. The veterans marched down in columns, plunged into the village without firing a shot, and in twenty minutes had swept every Prussian out of it, leaving it to be reoccupied by the Young Guard. Having thus, as he thought, cleared his right flank, Napoleon decided that the time was come for the final blow. He could see on his extreme right Durutte, already master of Papelotte and La Haie, preparing to ascend the slope, his own troops fighting strongly and with advantage in the centre, Hougoumont blazing on the left.

Waterloo: Evening

All seemed to be well; and after nearly eight hours of desperate fighting the supreme moment was at hand. He ordered Drouot to set nine battalions of the Guard in motion, keeping two at Plancenoit, and three in reserve; and he himself rode down to lead the foremost of them into the valley. Reille and d'Erlon were instructed to advance simultaneously, with such troops as they could raise, upon the centre and upon Hougoumont.

But there was one thing which Napoleon did not and could not see. Soon after six o'clock Ziethen, after endless delays both in starting and in marching, had arrived at Ohain with his advanced guard—perhaps five thousand men—and had been met by Colonel Freemantle of Wellington's staff with a pressing request for an immediate reinforcement, even if of no more than three thousand men. Ziethen hesitated to comply until his whole corps should have come up; and one of his staff-officers, galloping forward to judge of the reasonableness of Wellington's demand, found so many men, wounded and unwounded, making off, that he reported the British to be in retreat.

Shortly afterwards an order arrived from Blücher for the 1st Corps to join Bülow; and Ziethen naturally moved his troops in that direction. Müffling, however, perceiving him from a distance, galloped at the top of his speed to entreat him to join Wellington, and after much hesitation contrived to persuade him. But meanwhile much time had been lost; and the only advantage so far gained from Ziethen's arrival within two miles of Wellington's left was that Vivian had felt himself justified in quitting his post in rear of Smohain to reinforce the centre. It was not until the Imperial Guard was actually in motion towards the valley that Ziethen's leading troops at last debouched from Smohain. At the sight of them it seems that some of the French troops began to

THE ATTACK OF THE FRENCH GUARD.

Scale $\frac{1}{20000}$.

Ditmer

Brig

Guard

Ney

la Haye Sainte

Hougomont

1/3 G

4 G.

1/K

2/K

4 C.

B le Alliance

2/2 d

2/2 C.

1/1 G

2/1 G.

give way. The emperor rallied them in person and sent *aides-de-camp* flying to all parts of his line to announce the arrival of Grouchy.

Wellington during this interval had brought forward Chassé's Netherlandish divisions from Merbe Braine to take the place of the Brunswickers in rear of Maitland and Colin Halkett; and he was apprised of the coming attack by a royalist colonel of *cuirassiers* who galloped up to Colonel Colborne of the Fifty-Second and told him that Napoleon with his Guard would be upon them in half an hour. The duke rode down the line between the Brussels and Nivelles roads ordering all battalions to be ranked four deep; and in this formation the infantry lay down, to avoid the cannonade with which Napoleon preluded his final advance, and awaited the storm.

By this time six battalions of the Guard had reached the foot of the hollow. The emperor left one of them [1] on a slight eminence midway between Hougoumont and La Haye Sainte; and the remaining five were ordered to advance in echelon from the right, the 1st battalion of the 3rd Grenadiers leading, followed in succession by the 4th Grenadiers, 1st and 2nd battalions of the 3rd Chasseurs and a single battalion of the *Chasseurs*.

Formed each of them in a dense column with a frontage of seventy to eighty men and a depth of at least nine ranks, [1] the five battalions moved off in superb order with two guns loaded with grape in the intervals between them, five generals at their head, and Ney in front of all. Proceeding parallel to the Brussels road for some distance they found their front covered by d'Erlon's troops, which were engaged immediately to west of La Haye Sainte, and turned obliquely to the north-west, with the result that the right-hand battalion fell slightly to the rear of the rest. In this order they strode into the re-entrant angle formed by the British right centre.

By this time the Allied batteries in this quarter had suffered so much from loss of men and disabled guns that their fire had grown perceptibly weaker. Cleeves's and Kuhlmann's guns had actually retired to fetch ammunition; Mercer's had grouped themselves into a strange heap, the men being too much exhausted to run them forward after

---

1. 2/3rd Grenadiers.
2. Houssaye thinks that the Guard attacked in squares, and there is much evidence in favour of his contention. But although the fate of d'Erlon's corps may have suggested this formation, I think it more probable that the battalions were really formed in column of double companies, which would give them the frontage and depth above described.

each recoil; and nowhere was shot any too plentiful. Happily Chassé, a very fine soldier who had won a great reputation in the French Army, called up Van der Smissen's Netherlandish battery, which came galloping forward from the reserve, and unlimbering on the right of Lloyd opened a rapid fire immediately. The remainder fired round-shot and grape with all the energy of which their few harassed and weary gunners were capable; and the Imperial Guards were seen to bend under the stroke like corn smitten by the wind. Still they never for a moment gave way, though, as the five battalions continued to advance over the miry ground under a continual tempest of shot, they lost their correct intervals and distances.

The two right-hand battalions seem to have dropped somewhat in rear, the third and fourth battalions, reckoning from the right, united into one, and the left-hand battalion preserved its place slightly in rear of the centre. Hence, apparently, it was that the third and fourth battalions—the 3rd Chasseurs—were the first to come into action against Maitland's brigade of Guards. They could see nothing of the British line whatever except the guns, for all the redcoats were lying down; and they had approached to within twenty yards when Wellington at last said, "Now, Maitland! Now's your time!" Then the old story of the Peninsular battles was repeated. The Guards, four ranks deep, had a front of over two hundred and fifty men, the two columns of the Imperial Guard a front of perhaps one hundred and fifty. The red-coats poured in a volley from the two foremost ranks which tore the front and flanks of the French to tatters, and, with the two rearmost ranks to reload for them, continued to rain on their enemies a murderous shower of bullets. The senior French commanders fell among the first; their men staggered, uncertain what to do next; and the junior officers, instead of waving them forward to the charge, gave the order to deploy.

It was the old mistake of Albuera. Such an evolution in the face of such a fire at close range was impossible. The flank-companies tried to come forward, but involuntarily shrank back before the storm of bullets. Hesitation became unsteadiness, and unsteadiness turned to disorder. Wellington and Saltoun gave the word to charge, and the red-coats lowering their bayonets rushed forward and hurled their enemies in confusion before them.

Observing the progress of the Guards, Halkett threw forward the Thirty-Third and Sixty-Ninth to protect their left flank; and it was, apparently, while these two battalions were thus advanced that the two right-hand battalions of the French Guard approached Halkett's brigade. What happened at this point it is extremely difficult to ascertain. It seems that the ' French gave way before the first volley of the Thirtieth and Seventy-Third, much to the surprise of the British, [3] but that their guns continued to play upon the redcoats with deadly effect. In an evil moment some one gave the order for the two British battalions to face about and take shelter under a bank in rear; and the whole brigade rushed back in panic. For a short time they were so much crowded together that they could not move; but, by the exertions of Halkett and their officers, they speedily recovered themselves, and, backed by Chassé's Belgians, repelled a second attack, either of these same battalions of the Guard or of some of Donzelot's troops.

The whole incident is somewhat obscure, but it is certain that at this point of the Allied line there was great danger for a time; and it seems probable that the first recoil of the Guard before the British volleys was due either to its previous losses from Van der Smissen's guns, or to the sight of their comrades retiring before Maitland's Guards.

Maitland's brigade, indeed, was following up its success triumphantly; but, before it had advanced fifty yards, the brigadier observed the 4th Chasseurs—the left-hand battalion of the French array—coming up to the rescue of their comrades upon his right flank. He gave the word to retire, but his voice was lost in the din of battle, and the order came to his men in the shape of "Form Square." The flank-companies of his battalions accordingly doubled back to take their place in square. The officers, who saw the mistake, tried to set it right; and in the general bewilderment the whole brigade ran back, disordered by the incomplete manoeuvre, to its original station, where it halted instantly at the word of command and re-formed with perfect steadiness and calm.

Wellington, perceiving the mishap, ordered the Rifles of Adam's brigade to molest the flank of the 4th Chasseurs; but Colborne, anticipating him, led down the Fifty-Second, and formed it, four deep, along the whole length of its flank, to "make the column feel his fire." Whether the 3rd Chasseurs had rallied in rear of the 4th, or whether some of Reille's troops had come up and joined it, is uncertain; but it should appear that there was certainly more than one battalion opposed to Colborne. As he formed his array the French opened a fire upon him which brought down one hundred and fifty men; but his answering volley was crushing, and was followed by a charge with the

3. *Waterloo Letters.*

FORMATION OF THE 3RD DIVISION AT WATERLOO.

Adapted from Kennedy's 'Notes on the Battle of Waterloo.'

(Not drawn to scale.)

The 3rd British Division consisted of the
5th British Brigade.   2nd Brigade K.G.L.   1st Hanoverian Brigade.

N.B.—The skirmishers, as drawn by Gen. Kennedy, are plainly too close to the guns ;
they were down the slope about on a level with Haye Sainte.

bayonet, under which the French broke and gave way.

The Fifty-Second now continued their advance straight across the battlefield from west to east, gradually inclining to their right as the French turned instinctively towards their original position at La Belle Alliance. The Rifles and Seventy-First were hastening to form on their left and right; and Colborne, bethinking himself of his danger from a possible attack of cavalry, was disposed to halt. "No, no," shouted Wellington. "Go on; go on."

The duke was right. The defeat of the Guard had shaken the French in every part of the field. The long period of passive endurance was past, and the time for a general counter-attack was come. While the Imperial Guard was making its onslaught upon Wellington, part of Pirch I.'s corps had joined Blücher, who had promptly ordered a fresh assault upon Plancenoit. Ziethen in the meantime had beaten back Durutte, whose artillery had opened upon Smohain; and, as his infantry came up, drove him farther from La Haie and Papelotte. Wellington, leaving Colborne to take care of himself, ordered Vivian to move down across the scene of the conflict between the British and the Imperial Guard, so as to complete the discomfiture of the enemy, and then galloped, together with a single staff-officer, from Hougoumont to the left of his line to order a general advance. When he reached Kempt and Lambert and bade them move, Harry Smith, Lambert's brigade-major, was fain to ask in what direction the movement was to be, for there was for the moment a lull in the firing and the smoke was so thick that nothing could be seen.

"Right ahead, to be sure," answered the duke; and presently the smoke cleared away, and a gleam of light flashed down from the setting sun. The duke raised his hat high in air, and at his signal the redcoats stirred at last from the ground to which they had been rooted, and broke into a majestic advance.

Under this combined counter-attack of the British, Hanoverians, Netherlanders and Prussians, the French gave way at every point.[4] Whole battalions, which had been brought back from La Belle Alliance after being engaged, left their arms piled and ran away. Wellington's progress exposed Durutte's flank to the onset of Ziethen; the defeat of Durutte uncovered the flank of Lobau; and by a supreme effort Blücher drove the Guard, after a most noble and glorious resistance, from Plancenoit. All was now confusion except in the three squares of the Old Guard which Napoleon had held in reserve, and in the single

---

4. Lord Ellesmere's *Personal Recollections of Wellington*.

regiment of Horse-grenadiers. Vivian, after dispersing a mass of broken infantry, had charged and routed some cavalry that attempted to check him; and he now broke into one square of infantry and passed on, cutting down the fugitives by scores.

Vandeleur followed him; and it was left chiefly to Colborne and the artillery to deal with the squares of the Old Guard, which retreated steadily and in perfect order, frequently turning to bay. Shortly after nine Blücher and Wellington met near La Belle Alliance, and it was arranged that the Prussians should take up the pursuit. Vivian pleaded that his brigade was still fresh, but was met by the rejoinder that the British had done a hard day's work, and that he must put his men into bivouac. The energy and resource with which the Prussians pushed the pursuit has become a proverb; but indeed the panic was such that there was little attempt at a rally. Napoleon himself, after journeying for a short distance in his carriage, took to his horse again and so escaped capture.

Little effort was made to check the pursuers at the defile of Genappe; and, as no rear-guard had been formed, the task of the Prussian cavalry, lighted by the moon, was an easy one. Insatiable in their vengeance for many evils suffered since Jena, the Prussians pressed the fugitives hard. Several times the weary French tried to bivouac, to be roused up to renewed flight by the merest handful of men, indeed by the mere sound of trumpet or drum. The chase lay over the field of Quatre Bras, where the hideous spectacle of the still unburied dead struck the fugitives with fresh horror and panic. Not until he reached Frasnes did Gneisenau give the order to halt. The French Army that had fought at Waterloo had, as a military body, literally ceased to exist.

Merbe Braine

Hougomont

Mon Plaisir

BATTLE OF WATERLOO
at ¾ before 8 o'clock, p.m.
Scale

English.
Prussians
French.

BATTLE OF WATERLOO
at 5 min. past 8 o'clock p.m.
Scale ___ ½ ___ ½ ___ ½ Mile.

▨ ▨ ▧ •••• English.
▨ ▨ ▨ ⚬⚬⚬⚬ Prussians.
▨ ▨ ▨ ⚬⚬⚬⚬ French.

CHAPTER 10

Waterloo: Night

The Allied troops bivouacked on the ground that they had won, all except the Thirty-Third and Sixty-Ninth, weak young battalions which, having been cruelly tried both at Quatre Bras and Waterloo, had reached the limit of their endurance. Wellington himself rode back silently at a walk to Waterloo followed by the remnant of his staff, one and all "wearing rather the aspect of a funeral train than of victory in one of the most important battles ever fought." Between ten and eleven [1] he reached the inn where were his headquarters, and on dismounting patted his chestnut thoroughbred, Copenhagen, approvingly on the quarter.

The horse, who had carried his master for fourteen or fifteen hours and must have galloped more miles than are generally traversed in the longest day's hunting, lashed out with his near hind leg as if he had only just left the stable; and this was the last danger that was escaped by the duke on the 18th of June. He sat down to write his despatch; and later on, the first casualty-lists were brought to him. He listened as the long tale of names was read to him, and, before it was half rehearsed, broke down and cried. Fitzroy Somerset had been wounded by his side; two more of his personal staff, Canning and Gordon, had been killed; Barnes, the adjutant-general, Elley his deputy, and De Lancey, the quartermaster-general, had all of them been wounded, the last, as it proved, mortally.

Among the generals, Picton, who had been struck by a bullet at Quatre Bras but had concealed the hurt, William Ponsonby, Duplat and Christian Ompteda had been killed; Uxbridge, together with all four of his *aides-de-camp*, Cooke, Kempt, Pack, Colquhoun Grant,

---

1. Jackson (*With Wellington's Staff at Waterloo*) says after ten; the duke himself said, a year after the event (*Supp. Desp.* 10.), between eleven and twelve.

Adam and Colin Halkett, had been wounded. Out of fifty assistants in the departments of the adjutant and the quartermaster-general, two had been killed and thirteen wounded. Of sixteen officers commanding regiments of cavalry, three had been killed and seven wounded; of twenty-five commanders of battalions, one had been killed and eleven wounded. In the four squadrons of the Life Guards thirteen officers had fallen; in the King's Dragoon Guards eleven, in the Royals thirteen, in the Greys sixteen, in the Seventh Hussars twelve, and in the Fifteenth Hussars nine.

In the two battalions of the First Guards seventeen officers had been killed or wounded, besides fourteen at Quatre Bras; in the Coldstream ten, and in the Scots Guards twelve; in the Twenty-Third, ten; in the Twenty-Seventh, nine out of twenty present; in the Thirtieth, sixteen, besides two at Quatre Bras; in the Thirty-second, nine, besides twenty-two at Quatre Bras; in the Thirty-Third, nine, besides twelve at Quatre Bras; in the Fortieth, eleven; in the Fifty-Second, ten; in the Sixty-Ninth, six, besides five at Quatre Bras; in the Seventy-First, fourteen; in the Seventy-Third, seventeen, besides four at Quatre Bras; in the Seventy-Ninth, thirteen, besides seventeen at Quatre Bras; in the Ninety-second, six, besides twenty at Quatre Bras; and in the two battalions of the Ninety-Fifth, [2] thirty, besides four at Quatre Bras. Lastly, in the Royal Artillery, out of some eighty officers present, seven had been killed and fifteen wounded on the 16th and 18th, and among the slain was Major Norman Ramsay.

Nor had the men suffered less severely than the officers. In the Household Cavalry Brigade the non-commissioned officers and men killed and wounded numbered over one hundred and eighty; and some two hundred and thirty were missing, having been taken prisoners. In the Union Brigade the dead alone exceeded two hundred and fifty and the wounded were little short of three hundred. The Twelfth Light Dragoons had over one hundred and ten casualties of all ranks, and the Seventh Hussars over one hundred and fifty. In the infantry, the Second battalion of the First Guards lost nearly one hundred and fifty non-commissioned officers and men, and the Third battalion three hundred and twenty-four; so that the First Guards lost altogether at Quatre Bras and Waterloo not far from eleven hundred rank and file out of two thousand present, and not a single man of them taken prisoner. The Coldstream lost two hundred and eighty-two and

---

2. There were present the 1st battalion, six companies of the 2nd, two companies of the 3rd.

the Third Guards two hundred and fifteen rank and file out of about a thousand present, and escaped cheaply.

Of the brigades that had been engaged at Quatre Bras, Halkett's began the Battle of Waterloo with nineteen hundred and fifty bayonets and came out with fourteen hundred and thirty; Kempt's with nineteen hundred came out with just over thirteen hundred; Pack's with fourteen hundred came out with nine hundred and seventy-five. Among the individual battalions the Twenty-Eighth had since the 16th lost two-fifths of its numbers, the Royals and Thirty-Second one-half, the Forty-Second, Seventy-Ninth and Ninety-Second considerably more than one-half. The battalions that were engaged at Waterloo only did not suffer so severely, except the eight companies of the second and third battalions of Rifles, which lost nearly one-third, and the Twenty-Seventh, which, pent up in square by the cross-roads above La Haye Sainte, was cruelly punished without an opportunity of firing a shot in reply. Out of seven hundred rank and file of the Twenty-Seventh present no fewer than ninety-six were killed outright and three hundred and fifty wounded—a noble record of stubborn endurance.

The battalions of the German Legion and the Hanoverians had not escaped more lightly than the majority of the British, having most of them casualties varying from one-fourth to one-third of their strength; while the gaps in the 2nd Light Battalion of the Legion amounted very nearly to one man in two. The proportion of the fallen among the Brunswickers was on the whole slightly smaller, for, even reckoning their previous losses at Quatre Bras, there was not one in which the proportion of slain or hurt amounted to one-third of their strength. Nevertheless, among the eight battalions one showed nearly two hundred casualties, two over one hundred and seventy, and a fourth over one hundred and fifty.

Of the Netherlanders it is more difficult to speak. The Prince of Orange stated their casualties at about forty-two hundred for the three days of the 15th, 16th and 18th of June; half of which, roughly speaking, were returned as "killed or missing" and the other half as wounded. From another table it appears that nearly sixteen hundred of the forty-two hundred were missing, and over twelve hundred slightly wounded. As the whole number of the British missing in the two actions little exceeded six hundred, and the majority of these were taken prisoners in the wild charge of the Household and Union Brigades of cavalry, there is evidently something here which needs explanation.

However, the main point was that Wellington's army had lost in all close upon fifteen thousand men, or not far from a fourth of its numbers, and that none the less it must continue to advance. So worn out was every soul after the battle that the chief artillery officer never thought of collecting the captured guns, which with characteristic arrogance and dishonesty the Prussians promptly appropriated to themselves. In deference to Wellington's protests, however, they gave up half of these, which left one hundred and twenty-two pieces in the duke's hands. [3] A weary staff-officer rode out at one in the morning of the 19th, bearing a terse order for the troops to move to Nivelles at daylight; [4] and a few hours later the duke betook himself to Brussels to see to various matters.

A vast mass of stragglers of all nations had found their way to the city, some in charge of wounded men, more from unmixed solicitude for their own safety; and there were disorder and plundering among these gentry which needed suppression. Lastly, it was necessary to take some measures for the relief of the wounded and to detail a small party, both officers and men, from every regiment which had suffered heavily, to look after them. In Brussels the duke stayed until the 20th, when he drove over in his curricle, wearing plain clothes, to join his army at Nivelles. The ground was still covered with the dead, and many French wounded were still lying among them, who bore their sufferings with admirable patience and received any help that could be given them with touching courtesy.

On the night of the 18th Bülow's corps of the Prussian Army halted at Genappe, and Ziethen's on the Charleroi road a mile or two south of Plancenoit; while three brigades of Pirch I.'s corps marched for Wavre to the assistance of Thielmann. The last-named officer had been attacked by Grouchy late in the afternoon of the 18th, but had held his own fairly well against odds of two to one until nightfall. On the 19th, Grouchy, having checked a counterattack, pressed Thielmann steadily backward along the Louvain road until in the course of the forenoon he heard of the result of the Battle of Waterloo, whereupon he resolved to retreat at once to Namur. Pirch I., who had reached Mellery on the 19th, pursued from thence on the 20th, and Thielmann likewise; but the French reached Namur with little loss, and Grouchy, crossing the Meuse, reached Philippeville on the 21st, and went on his way unmolested.

3. Basil Jackson, *With Wellington's Staff at Waterloo.*
4. *Ibid.*

CHAPTER 11

The Pursuit

The main armies of Blücher and Wellington marched on the 19th and following days, the former by Charleroi, Avesnes, Etroeung and Fesmy, the latter by Nivelles, Binche and Valenciennes, halting for a day on the 23rd. Le Quesnoi and Valenciennes were blockaded by Wellington's troops, Landrecies and Maubeuge by the Prussians; and it was decided by the two commanders to advance to Paris by the right bank of the Oise, as the defeated enemy were said to be assembling at Laon and Soissons. On the 24th Blücher resumed his march, having been joined by Thielmann's corps, while Wellington halted at Le Cateau to await the arrival of his pontoon-trains. On the 23rd he had detached Colville's division and a few more troops to Cambrai, which had carried the place by escalade with trifling loss; [1] and the town was set apart for the residence of King Louis, who had re-entered France from Ghent.

On the 26th the Prussian advanced guard reached Compiègne, and Wellington's army was between Vermand and Péronne. This last place, being fully fortified, refused to surrender; and the Guards were detached to storm it. The light companies crossed the drawbridge and blew open the gate, whereupon the governor speedily agreed to a capitulation. On the 27th Grouchy with a part of his army engaged the Prussians at Compiègne, but, finding himself outnumbered, fell back. He engaged them again on the 28th, and ultimately on the 29th entered Paris, before the north side of which the whole of the Prussians encamped that evening. Negotiations for an armistice had already been opened with Wellington by commissioners from the capital, but had been rejected until Napoleon should quit Paris, which on this same day he did.

But even so, Paris was not yet taken, and Wellington considered

---

1. Eight killed, twenty-nine wounded. The troops engaged were the British battalions of Colville's division.

an attack with the forces at his disposal very hazardous. [2] The French troops, with the help of the lines thrown up on the heights from Montmartre to Belleville, could still have checked the advance of the Allies; and it was therefore resolved to send the Prussians round to the south side of the city, which was unfortified.

Accordingly on the 30th of June and the two following days the Prussians marched round, not without some sharp fighting both on the 1st and 2nd of July; Wellington moved his troops into the places vacated by the Prussians; and on the 3rd, in consequence of overtures from the Provisional Government, a convention was signed under which the Allies agreed to suspend hostilities upon the surrender of Paris, and the French Army retired to the Loire.

It was no doubt a relief to Wellington to be quit of the campaign without more fighting, for, if he had thought ill of his army before Waterloo, he thought still worse of it after, when all the best of the men had been killed or disabled. From want of carriages and drivers he could not carry with him one-fourth of the necessary ammunition; and his staff, its most efficient members having been slain or hurt, was useless.

Above all, the behaviour of the Netherlanders, now the greatest part of the army, was infamous. Neither officers nor men would stay with their companies on the march. They wandered from house to house, not excepting Wellington's own headuarters, robbing, destroying and plundering, forcing the sentries, rescuing the prisoners, and committing every description of outrage. In fact, they were simply a rabble, and for military purposes valueless. Wellington at daybreak of the 26th had ordered a brigade of the Netherlandish infantry to Péronne to support the assault. They arrived at nine o'clock in the evening, an hour after the Guards had taken the place; but a few Belgian cavalry were on the spot, who, after the capitulation was signed, cut the ropes of the drawbridge and broke violently into the town.

The British staff-officer, who had arranged the terms, ordered them out, whereupon the ruffians tried to cut him down, and the French governor was actually obliged to draw his sword to protect him. The Belgian soldier, properly disciplined and led by good officers, has deservedly won high reputation on many fields; but in 1815 he was neither disciplined nor controlled, and it is idle to pretend that such levies were of any military worth.

Such incidents as these prove that the contemporary narratives of Belgian misbehaviour at Waterloo are absolutely true, and they are

2. Wellington's Despatch to Blücher, 2nd July 1815.

BATTLE OF WAVRE
at 4 o'clock a.m.
19ᵗʰ JUNE

Scale of one mile.

■ ▥ ╫ •••• Prussians.
▣ ▦ ╫ ○○○○ French.

Lasne Stream

Genval

Rixansart

Bourgeois

SPENCER

BLÜCHER

SPARKE

St
Lambert

ZIEGLER

PAJOL

STROLE

Preslong Sart

Grand
Sart

Roffe Sart

S. Robert

Cornet

Touchant

Touchart

BATTLE OF WAVRE

at 4 o'clock p.m.
18th June.
Scale.

0   ½   1   2

Miles.

Prussians ⬛ ⬛ ⬛⬛ ⬛ French

Bajidet

Genval

Frischermont

Rixansart

Bourgeois

del Brire

Deadbremont

To Planchenoit

Pajean

St. Lambert

Roffe

St. Robert

Hanolelet

Lasne

Cornet

Touchan

Pind

To Planchenoit

Remveau

Rosieres

Barriere

Stadt

Louis Delotte

Cambre

Le Marche

Bas Wavre

Stream

Hopital

PAVAL

Henri de Jour

JACOB

Bien

BRUCE

RECHON

des Delhou

Prefond Sart

Grand Sart

Limate

Sart

Bierg

Trois Dehouz

Louvrang

le Mont

Limelette

L'Auzel

R. Dyle

la Bacherie

not to be refuted by specious apologies proffered after the convenient lapse of a century. It is, however, fair to add that the Prussians behaved as ill or worse, both before and after the capitulation of Paris. They had, it is true, old scores to pay off, but this was no excuse for behaving, as Wellington put it, like children, he wrote:.

> Among the officers of the Allied troops the strongest objections are entertained to anything like discipline and order

And this defect caused him not only disgust but not a little alarm. he wrote to Castlereagh on the 14th of July:

> If one shot were fired in Paris the whole country will rise against us.[3]

On the 6th of July the Prussians occupied Paris, while Wellington's army stayed outside. Blücher wished to levy a huge contribution and, from mere rage at the name, to blow up the bridge of Jena. Wellington dissuaded him from the former project until the Allied Sovereigns should arrive, and meanwhile posted a British sentry on the bridge. This did not prevent the old marshal from trying to blow it up, British sentry and all; but the Prussian engineers failed on the Seine as they had failed on the Sambre from sheer ignorance of their business.

And then came the bitter battle of the diplomatists on the terms of peace; Prussia and the. German States clamouring for the dismemberment of France and for a gigantic indemnity; the Tsar, Castlereagh and Wellington, and later Metternich, standing up strenuously against them. On the 20th of November peace was at last signed. France agreed to the cession of Condé, Givet, Charlemont, Philippeville, Mariembourg, Sarrelouis, and Landau, and to the dismantling of Huningen. The indemnity to be paid by her was fixed at twenty-eight millions sterling; and it was arranged that for five years an army of one hundred and fifty thousand men [8] should occupy certain places in France at France's ex-

3. *Wellington's Despatches.* To Castlereagh, 14th July; to the King of the Netherlands, 18th July; to Bathurst and to Sir H. Wellesley, 20th July; to Torrens, 1st Aug. 1815.

4.

English, Headquarters Cambrai	. . .	30,000
Wurtemburgers, Headquarters Weissenberg	. .	5,000
Russians, Headquarters Maubeuge	. . .	30,000
Danes, Headquarters Lewarde	. . . .	5,000
Prussians, Headquarters Sedan	. . . .	30,000
Hanoverians, Headquarters Tourcoing	. .	5,000
Austrians, Headquarters Colmar	. . .	30,000
Saxons, Headquarters Condé	. . . .	5,000
Bavarians, Headquarters Pont-a-Mousson	. .	10,000

pense, the whole being under the command of the Duke of Wellington, with headquarters at Cambrai, for the term of occupation.

Martinique and Guadeloupe, which had been occupied in June and August by General Leith, the former bloodlessly, the latter after a little fighting which cost the British about seventy killed and wounded, [5] were both of them restored to France.

So ended this long and desolating war; and it remains only to recount briefly the fate of some of the principal actors therein, and to review the final campaign. Murat, in a fit of madness, disembarked on the coast of his lost kingdom and was captured and shot on the 13th of October. Ney having been arrested and condemned to death, was shot on the 5th of December. He had sought the honourable end, that was his due, a thousand times throughout the long agony of Waterloo; but the cruel fate which killed five horses under him reserved the rider for the bullets of a French firing-party. He lives immortal as the bravest of the brave. Soult fled after Waterloo and remained in banishment until 1819, when he began a new career in the service of France. Of him, as of Marmont and of Victor, we may perhaps hear again. Massena, worn out by work and wounds, died in 1817. He will always be remembered in England as the general who, even in the years of his decadence, never failed to appear where Wellington least wanted to see him, and evoked the unstinted admiration of the entire British Army by the masterly skill of his retreat from before Torres Vedras.

Napoleon himself, after leaving Paris on the 29th of June, set out for Rochefort with some idea of sailing for America. He reached the port on the 3rd of July, and, yielding to the pressure of the Provisional Government, embarked on the 8th. For some days he waited, forbidden to set foot again in France and yet not daring to put to sea in face of the British cruisers; and on the 13th he wrote his well-known letter of surrender to the Prince Regent. The original document lies before me as I write, the text in the hand of some amanuensis, firmly written but containing one grammatical error, the signature bold and far more legible than usual, as if to mark with dignity the close of a transcendently great career.

On the 15th he embarked on board the *Bellerophon* and was carried to Torbay. There had been wild talk of putting him to death; and Liverpool wrote flatly that he wished the King of France would hang or shoot him, as the best termination of the business; but Wellington

---

5 The troops engaged were the 63rd, York Chasseurs, West India Rangers, and York Rangers. The 63rd had 25 casualties.

had no intention of playing the part of hangman, and the British Government had no idea of calling upon him to do so. Since, however, it was necessary for the peace of Europe that he should be kept in safe custody, it fell to England, as practically the only possessor of distant islands and of a fleet that could ensure their safety, to take charge of him. He claimed the right to live quietly in England; and, a rumour having got abroad that he was to be sent to Fort George at the mouth of the Inverness Firth, the Inverness Local Militia joyfully volunteered to act as his guard. [6] But before the end of July his place of confinement had been determined, and sailing in the king's ship *Northumberland* he landed on the 16th of October at St. Helena.

At the pitiful spectacle of a great genius descending to occupy itself with the pettiest of petty tricks, intrigues, and mischiefs I am not minded even to glance. I have as little wish to study the vast fabric of lies, misstatements, misrepresentations and calumnies that the idle hands at St. Helena took such pains to rear to the honour, as their littleness conceived it, of their royal martyr, and to the shame of his honest and upright custodian. Least of all would I call to remembrance the degrading use to which Whig politicians turned the name, which had made all Europe tremble, to the despicable ends of party strife. It is enough that Napoleon ended his life, by his own choice, without dignity and without resignation. Though a very great captain and a very great administrator, he was always an adventurer and, after his rise to supreme power, always a gambler. From 1803 onward he was continually playing double or quits until he had exhausted the favours of fortune; and, when she turned against him and all hope was gone, he could not school himself to accept her buffets with a smile.

On the 5th of May 1821 the end came, and he was carried to his grave by twelve grenadiers of the Twentieth Foot, no unworthy bearers, for some of them had faced the brave soldiers of Imperial France at Maida, Vimeiro, Coruña, Vitoria, in the bitterest fights of the Pyrenees, at Orthez and at Toulouse.

★★★★★★

The campaign of Waterloo has been made the subject of whole libraries of books in all languages, and has been subjected to examination so microscopic as to be without parallel in military history. The reasons are readily found. The story is alluring in the first place, because it is that of the end of a great European cataclysm, and be-

---

6. Record Office, H.O. Internal Defence, 322. Lt.-Col. Rose to Sec. of State, 1st Aug. 1815.

cause the last act of the drama brought all the foremost actors of the time upon the stage. But its greatest attraction is that it only lasted four days, and may therefore be exhausted with a comparatively small amount of labour. Whether the excessive toil expended upon it has really made it clearer and more intelligible than other campaigns, may well be doubted.

Writers have too often approached it with some ulterior object, to illustrate some theory of war or strategy, to glorify the share taken by their own nation or even by their own regiment, to explain the defeat of Napoleon, to minimise the success of Wellington, to exalt one commander, to abase another, to prove that, if something had not happened, the result would have been very different, and so forth. To such mistreatment many, indeed the majority, have added the mistake of regarding it as an isolated event, whereas, to take one detail only, it is impossible for one who has not deeply studied Graham's campaign of 1814 in the Netherlands, to understand how bad Wellington's troops really were. But, after all the study and research expended upon the four days of the 15th to the 18th of June 1815, and the new material which it has produced, it must be confessed that the literature of Waterloo is more prolific of new conjectures than of new facts.

We know that certain orders were issued on both sides, and that certain messages were sent and delivered. But what other orders or messages, verbal or in writing, may have passed, when the said messages were despatched, when they were delivered, and whether the watches in the French, Prussian, British, and Netherlandish Armies kept uniform time or varied by half-an-hour, we do not know and shall never know. Wellington warned aspirant historians against inquiring too much, on the ground that such a course would lead to bewilderment rather than truth; and he was quite right.

The main facts are simple enough. Napoleon with one hundred and twenty-five thousand men set out to fight Blücher and Wellington with two hundred and fifty thousand. The two latter had dispersed their armies in cantonments over a very wide front, and Napoleon hoped by stepping in between them to beat them in detail before they could unite, and indeed before either of their armies could be fully concentrated in itself. The first stage, that is to say, the work of the 15th of June, may be called completely successful. Everything indeed did not pass exactly as Napoleon had designed—that is the rule rather than the exception in war—but it may be said that the British and Prussian commanders were surprised on the 15th. In the details of their concentration bad mistakes were made both by the Prussian staff and by the British commander; but the worst mistake of the latter was set right by his Netherlandish subordinates, Constant and Perponcher, who saw the importance of clinging to Quatre Bras.

On the 16th it was Napoleon who was surprised. He expected to reach Gembloux on one side and Brussels on the other without serious fighting, and he found himself set down to two pitched battles. It is urged with justice that, if d'Erlon's corps had not been kept walking to and fro all day between the two battlefields, the issue might have been very different; and a vast deal of ingenuity has been expended to account for d'Erlon's conduct. But the explanation is very simple. D'Erlon was badly needed upon both battlefields owing to the huge initial superiority of the Allies over the French in the matter of numbers.

The emperor had misread the entire situation, and had confused all his commanders by imposing his misreading upon them. Yet even so Napoleon was fortunate in the fact that Blücher chose a bad position and occupied it vilely; for Ligny, or the equivalent to Ligny, would have resulted very differently if Wellington had been in command of the Prussian Army. On the other hand, it was unlucky for the emperor that Wellington was in command at Quatre Bras, for no other general could have handled the early stage of that critical action with such consummate skill, and no troops but the British, fighting under his command, could have made so stubborn a resistance in the face of so heavy punishment.

At nightfall on the 16th, therefore, Napoleon had lost a great number of men and had accomplished very little. The Prussians had indeed been beaten, but not very severely; and though ten thousand soldiers of the corps that had suffered most heavily had dispersed, there was one more corps which had been little engaged, and another that had not been engaged at all. It suited Napoleon's preconceived ideas to assume that the Prussians were retreating, without thought of further contest, to the eastward, and that five-and-thirty thousand men would be sufficient, if not to hunt them beyond any sphere of usefulness, at any rate to hold them in check until he should have disposed of Wellington. But here we find the confusion of thought due principally to imperfect intelligence, which vitiated every measure taken by Napoleon after the initial stage of the campaign. Thirty-five thousand were fewer than were necessary to paralyse the Prussians if they were not thoroughly beaten, but more than were necessary to keep them running if they were.

On the French left wing Ney has been much blamed for not attacking Wellington earlier, in order to make his retreat difficult if not impossible. But it is plain that Ney was thoroughly bewildered by the course which events had taken. An easy, almost unopposed, march to Brussels had been prescribed to him in the first instance, instead of which he had been stopped before he had advanced two miles, and had only been able to hold his ground with great difficulty and serious loss. He could not fail to infer that the emperor had made grave miscalculations at the very outset of the campaign, that his plans would need revision. The marshal had received a great many contradictory commands on the 16th, and the general result had not been satisfactory.

The Allied armies were, according to Napoleon's design, to have run away in different directions as soon as the French host appeared; but they had not run away. They had fought desperately, though disunited. One of them had held its ground, and the defeat of the other had not been even reported to Ney until twelve hours after the event. A signal success does not generally take so long to make itself known; and Ney may well have had his doubts as to the plight of the right wing. There were, in fact, signs of uncertainty and hesitation in the mind of the commander-in-chief, easily intelligible in one who had started to fight against an army of twice his own strength, but not calculated to inspire his subordinates with confidence.

The thunderstorm on the 17th was a complication decidedly in favour of the Allies; but, if we are to go back over past campaigns and alter the weather from day to day, we shall only lose ourselves in unprofitable conjectures. It was open to Napoleon to turn the bulk of his force upon Wellington at Quatre Bras quite early in the morning of the 17th; and, if he had done so, it is probable that no weather could have saved the campaign from ending very differently. But he did not do so, and when at last he made up his mind to fling himself upon Wellington's rear-guards, it was too late. Meanwhile it is to be noted that the chance of catching Wellington at a disadvantage was due to the neglect of Blücher's staff to apprise the Duke of the Prussian retreat after Ligny. But war is a chapter of accidents; and any other campaign, if put under the microscope, would show as many as that of Waterloo.

The most remarkable point in the whole story is Wellington's nerve in accepting battle with a very bad army, before he had actually effected his junction with Blücher. It is not impossible that he was prompted thereto by the desire to choose his position for himself and to defend it according to his own ideas, after experience of the Prussian dispositions at Ligny. Yet he took a tremendous risk, for the best of his troops had been very roughly handled at Quatre Bras, and the worst were so bad—not because they were cowards, but because they had no heart in their work—that no reliance could be reposed upon them. The excellent battalions of the German Legion were from the first lamentably weak in numbers; the best of the British had been very seriously diminished by their losses at Quatre Bras; and the Hanoverians and Brunswickers, the latter of whom had also suffered considerably, were very young and raw. Altogether, reckoning only the troops which he could trust, more or less, he engaged Napoleon at the odds of two against three.

In the matter of guns Napoleon had the advantage of about eight pieces to five in numbers, and of weight of metal into the bargain, for the emperor, it will be recalled, had several batteries of twelve-pounders, whereas the duke had nothing heavier than nine-pounders. Everything, therefore, was in Napoleon's favour, except that he was opposed to a strange enemy, whom it pleased him to assume to be similar to all other enemies that he had met. He did not realise that he was matched against a commander who, in the actual direction of a battle, was his equal if not his superior; that the British infantry was as tenacious as the Russian, but far more active and far more formidable with the musket; and that both the commander and his troops had been well schooled by experience to meet the somewhat crude tactical methods of the French Army.

The details of the battle itself, except in its broad lines, are, as usual, so much complicated by conflicting narratives as to defy all attempt to unravel them. It is impossible even to be perfectly sure of the number of battalions of the Imperial Guard which took part in the final attack, much less of their formation and of the portion of the Allied line that was struck by any particular battalion. Only staff-officers can ever catch a general view of any action; a great number of these were killed or wounded in the course of the day upon both sides, so that they could only give either imperfect narratives or no narratives at all; and all witnesses agree that the smoke was so dense that the regimental officers always, and the staff-officers for the most part, were working in the dark.

However, Napoleon pursued his usual method of making a great bustle from end to end of his enemy's line, so as to bewilder him as to the true point of the attack; but it was a new thing to him to fight against an enemy which, as a tactical principle, was kept out of his sight, according (to quote the words of General Foy) to the excellent custom of the English. It may well be, therefore, that he had his own share of bewilderment. Be that as it may, it is certain that his attacks were incoherent—what he would have called *décousus*—though this was a fault which, in general, his worst enemies would have hesitated to attribute to him.

We may therefore set down to his subordinates the blunder which converted the advance against Hougoumont from a secondary into a primary operation. But the onslaught of d'Erlon's corps upon the centre, which was really the most serious movement of the whole day, might surely have merited some little personal attention from the general-in-chief. There were at least three French generals in the field who could have warned Napoleon that an attack upon British infantry in line by battalions in close column, without space to deploy, had again and again been tried and found wanting. It is true that the assault was finally routed by a charge of British cavalry; but this too might have been foreseen since the day of Salamanca. There can be little doubt, I think, that this charge had its effect upon the French infantry all through the day. Nothing serious was attempted over the scene of the Union Brigade's attack; and, according to many good authorities, the Imperial Guard did not venture to make its final advance except in squares.

After the failure of d'Erlon, came the great mistake of attacking unbroken infantry with cavalry only, an idea which apparently was instilled into the brain of Ney by the sight of British battalions retiring from the crest of the hill to the reverse slope. This blunder on Ney's part and its disastrous consequence must be placed to the credit of Wellington and of the unseen array which he alone among his contemporaries employed when defending a position. Last came the most trying ordeal of all for the Allies—incessant raids of cavalry and infantry, sometimes supported by cannon at close range, and launched at many different points upon the British squares after a pitiless rain of shot and shell from Napoleon's massed batteries.

The constancy and steadfastness of British, Hanoverians and Brunswickers under this trial, especially after the capture of La Haye Sainte had enabled the French to enfilade a part of their line, was beyond all praise. More than one battalion broke, and indeed ran, when brought

CAMPAIGN OF 1815
Operations
AFTER
18th June.

Oudenarde
R. Scheldt
Gra
Tournay
Condé
Valenciennes
Quesnoy
Englefontaine
Doullens
Cambray
Le Cateau
Bapaume
Serain
Fesmy
Premont
Peronne
Guise
R.
Amiens
R. Somme
Vermand
St Quentin
Origny
Essigny
Ham
Cerizy
R serre
Montdidier
Roye
Guiscard
La Fere
Crevecœur
Chauny
Beauvais
R Oise
Lao
Compiègne
Clermont
Soissons
R.
St Martin Longeau
Pont St Maxence
Villecourt
Creil
Fleurines
Crepy
Villers Cotteret
Senlis
Mont l'eveque
La Ferté Milon
Chantilly
Nanteuil
La Chapelle
R Ourcq
R M
Pontoise
Marly la Ville
Dammartin
Château Thierry
Vanderlan
Gonesse
Blancmenil
Gernevez
Le Bourget
Auberviliers
Montmorail
St Germain
Montmorency
Bocquencourt
Belleville
Versailles
PARIS
Clamart

Alost

BRUSSELS • Louvain

Tirlemont • St Trond

Tongres

mmont

R Dender

Hal?

Rhode • Ste Agathe

R Senne

Waterloo

R Dyle

Wavre

Ath

Maison du Roi

Braun

Hannut

LEIGE

Nivelles

Genappe • Mellery

Baisy

Gembloux

Sombreffe

Ligny

Mons

Binche

Fme l'Eveque

Anderlues

Quatre Bras

R Meuse

Namur

Huy

R Sambre

Charleroi

Maubeuge

Walcourt

Franco Belgian Frontier 1815

Collerel

Beaumont

Dinant

Ciney

Philippeville

Avesnes

Givet

Etreux

Mortemburg

Chimay

R Meuse

Rocroi

Couvins

Vervins

Mezieres

N

Aisne

Rethel

Reims

R Vesle

arne

Epernay

Chalons sur Marne

into the fighting-line under that terrible fire. But they rallied and came back; for, wherever weakness was, there by magic appeared Wellington, perfectly calm and collected, inspiring all with confidence and fortitude. He said himself that he personally had saved the battle four times, and, if he had said forty times, he would not have overstated the truth. The men would have been glad enough to advance.

What they found so hard to endure was the incessant fire of artillery to which they could make no answer. But they were bidden to stand, and, with Wellington to command them, they did stand. The miracles wrought by his presence and personality among a host of raw troops throw into the background the amazing patience and firmness with which, through hours of awful anxiety, he bided his time and forbade any movement until the Prussians should come up. Much is justly made of Blücher's exhortation to his troops to enable him to keep his promise to Wellington. Too little is said and thought of the silent influence and example by which Wellington infused ever fresh courage into a thin line of wavering recruits, and fairly forced them to keep his promise to Blücher. Without his presence and that of the officers and men whom he had taught to meet the legions of France, not only without fear, but with full confidence of victory, Waterloo had been lost.

The final issue of the day was of course decided, as Wellington was the first to acknowledge, by the advent of the Prussians, which was due wholly to the energy of Blücher. With proper management they should have arrived on the field at two; as things fell out, they did not appear until half-past four and did not make their presence seriously felt until seven. But they won their way through Plancenoit only by strenuous and desperate fighting, which cost them between six and seven thousand killed and wounded and missing. Their casualties, in actual fact, actually exceeded those of the British, strictly so called; as well they might, for they had many more troops present;[7] and a comparison of the casualty lists sets forth some curious details.

The British officers killed numbered eighty-three, the Prussian twenty-two; the British officers wounded three hundred and sixty-three, the Prussian two hundred and eighty-six. The tale of the pri-

---

7. The British engaged at Waterloo (Wellington *Supp. Desp.* 10) numbered 23,991 rank and file, or, adding one-eighth for other ranks, roughly 27,000 men. Bülow's corps at the opening of the campaign numbered 30,000 and Pirch I.'s 31,000. Deducting one-third from these figures as a handsome allowance for casualties and absentees, there are left at least 40,000 men.

vates is as follows: killed, of the British twelve hundred and forty-five, of the Prussians eleven hundred and twenty-two; wounded, of the British forty-two hundred and sixty-one, of the Prussians thirty-eight hundred and sixty-nine; missing, of the British five hundred and fifty-eight, of the Prussians thirteen hundred and five. These figures do honour to both parties, but leave little doubt upon whom the brunt of the fighting fell; though the credit for one of the most successful pursuits in military history belongs wholly to the Prussians, and in particular to Gneisenau.

The losses of the French were appalling. The only means of judging them are from the published lists of the fallen officers, which are most pitiful to read. Never did the French soldier cover himself with greater glory than at Waterloo, his persistent gallantry in attack being beyond all praise. The weak point of the Army was its indiscipline. A large proportion of the men were old soldiers, very many of them released prisoners from various countries. They had not had time to settle down under the rule of their idolised leader; and, as they themselves had restored him, they and the junior officers were inclined to look upon themselves as the real masters of the situation. The general officers had many of them reconciled themselves with the Bourbons. They were sick of war. They pined for a little peace and quiet and, being of longer sight than the men, doubted the issue of Napoleon's usurpation.

Thus there was some suspicion in the lower ranks towards the higher, and no perfect sympathy between them. This probably accounted for the incoherent nature of the principal attacks both in general and in detail. If one general hung back, from reasons of sound military prudence, another in his heart accused him of treason and hurried him on. So too in the charges of the French cavalry, every squadron-leader took matters into his own hands and attacked upon his own account, fearful lest his colonel should be lukewarm in the fight; and thus there was no grand overwhelming onslaught made at any time in the day.

Hence, when the Prussians arrived upon the field in force instead of Grouchy, as the emperor had announced, there was a general cry of treachery; and the army, saving a few choice regiments, fell into dissolution. Discipline was always the weak side of the Napoleonic armies, and at Waterloo the defect proved fatal. None the less the French approved themselves most noble fighting-men.

There has been much speculation as to the possible issue of the fight if the Prussians had failed to arrive on the field. This is hardly profitable, because Wellington only accepted battle on the understanding that Blücher would support him; and we have seen how loyally both chiefs stood by their agreement. There can be no doubt that many even of the better Allied troops had been tried almost to the limit of their endurance, and that there were others besides the Netherlanders who quitted the field without the Netherlanders' excuse. Wellington in a letter to Lord Mulgrave six months after the battle declared himself ill-pleased with the conduct of the Artillery, alleging that, instead of taking refuge in the squares when the French cavalry charged, they ran off the field, taking with them limbers, ammunition and everything. The Royal Regiment has never forgiven the duke for this letter, which indeed seems to be one of those sweeping indictments to which the great man was too much prone in moments of impatience.

Whether there was one unfortunate battery which so misconducted itself, and, if so, which battery it was; or whether the whole accusation arose out of some mistake, some misconception or some misrepresentation, it is impossible to say. Wellington averred that, when the French cavalry fell back, there were no artillery to fire at them; but I can find no evidence of this, though plenty against it. Altogether it seems to me that this letter must be set aside as too hasty to be accurate.

There was some complaint also of the Light Cavalry on the right wing. Uxbridge rode up to the Guards of Maitland's brigade and said:

Well done, men. By God, we stand on you. If I could only get my fellows to do the same! But by God, they won't budge—but I'll try again.

The writer to whom we owe this detail [8] adds that the Light Cavalry in that part of the field were of little profit, partly because they were brought up for small isolated attacks instead of in a mass. This, however, is quite unconfirmed, rather indeed contradicted, by other authorities; and it is probable that Uxbridge was speaking of some of the foreign cavalry which, it is well known, refused to follow him.

In the infantry, as we have seen, there was at one moment a panic in Halkett's brigade which, however, soon gave place to order. Much has been written about the number of fugitives, chiefly, but by no means exclusively, Netherlanders, that thronged the road to Brussels; but this is due, I think, to the facts that the number of wounded was very great, and that there was more than the usual number of spectators in the rear of the army. Craufurd had much the same story to tell

8. MS. Journal of Colonel James Stanhope.

when he came up to Talavera.

On the whole, therefore, I doubt whether the Allies were so much shaken at the close of the battle as French writers have been disposed to think. Up to the very end the French skirmishers tried in vain to tempt the British squares to fire a volley at them which might give a chance to the French battalions to charge while the British muskets were empty. A few picked marksmen alone answered the sharpshooters, and the remainder coolly waited for the word of command to fire.[9] Troops that, after hours of harassing attack by all three arms, are still so perfectly under control cannot be considered shaken.

It must be noticed too that, owing to Wellington's admirable husbandry of his reserves, he had still, before the French attacks ceased, Vandeleur's and Vivian's brigades of cavalry, two battalions of Mitchell's brigade of infantry and the Hanoverian brigades of Vincke and Best practically untouched, while the Fourth and Fortieth regiments of Lambert's brigades, the former fresh from work in America, had suffered indeed considerable loss, but nothing so serious as to impair their righting powers. Colonel James Stanhope, who had exceptionally good opportunities for forming a judgment, thought that even without the Prussians the Allies would have held their ground, and made their final short advance to La Belle Alliance on the 18th; but he admitted that it was doubtful whether the French or the Allies would have retreated on the 19th.

Had Wellington retreated, the Forest of Soignes was easily traversable by troops of all arms, and the border would have made a good defensible position for the rear-guard. Whether Stanhope's opinion were correct or not, it is impossible to say and unprofitable to argue. All that can certainly be said is that, when the battle ended, both armies were rapidly reaching the end of their powers, and that the ammunition of the French artillery was failing, [10] The French had endeavoured at the outset to carry matters forward with a rush, and their failure had cost them very dear. Thenceforward their efforts, though rather more methodical, had still for various reasons continued to be incoherent.

---

9. Stanhope tells an amusing story which illustrates the perennial strife between staff-officers and regimental officers. Captain Horace Seymour, one of Uxbridge's *aides-de-camp*, seeing that the Guards left the fire of the French skirmishers unanswered, galloped up to Lord Saltoun and said, "G—d d—n you, don't you see those are French! Why don't you fire at them?" To which Saltoun replied, "Why, d— n you, don't you think we know better when to fire than you do!" Seymour thereupon vanished.

10. *Vie militaire du General Foy.*

The emperor appears never to have had complete control of the battle; and an army, whatever its valour, which goes its own way in a fight, may collapse suddenly at any moment. In any case, if the Prussians had not come up and Napoleon had defeated Wellington, only a very small fragment of the French army would have been fit for further work; and it is questionable whether Napoleon would have ventured to meet Blücher, who, it may be presumed, would have made things very unpleasant for Grouchy. Had the emperor again engaged the Prussians, even successfully, he would have been left with nothing to meet the advance of the main body of the Allies; and Paris would have been occupied in August or September instead of in July.

On the whole it may be said that Napoleon set out to achieve the impossible, and that his task was so heavy and so difficult that it was too much even for his skill and for his powers. It has been pleaded that he was no longer at his best, and that he was seriously hampered by the loss of Berthier as the chief of his staff. But no man is always at his best; and Wellington was equally without his old and tried staff-officer, George Murray. Wellington also was not at his best, otherwise he would not have left sixteen thousand men at Hal during the battle. This last matter constitutes a mystery which will never be cleared up, for Wellington was not the man deliberately to leave so large a force idle, though within call of the battlefield, unless there had been some reason which in his judgment was of overpowering importance. Blücher and Gneisenau were not at their best, otherwise they would not have accepted battle in so bad a position as that of Ligny.

It may account in part for their mistakes that not one of the three armies, French, Prussian and Anglo-German, was really a good one, all alike having been hastily scraped together, with imperfect organisation and a large proportion of raw troops in the ranks. But there were three great leaders at their head, and under them half-trained troops became heroes. Napoleon was out-generalled and out-fought; but for no other man would the French horse and foot have dashed themselves so incessantly against the line of death on the heights of Mont St. Jean. Blücher's army had been defeated in a very hard fight, and himself, aged seventy-two, ridden over and cruelly battered by galloping squadrons. The old man revived himself partly by strange remedies, [11] more by his own unconquerable spirit, and heartened his

---

11. He dosed himself with gin and onions; and on approaching Hardinge directly afterwards observed, no doubt with truth, "*Ich stinke etwas.*" Stanhope. *Conversations of the Duke of Wellington.*

men to those superhuman exertions which brought them and their guns, late indeed but in time, to the field of Waterloo.

Lastly, it must be repeated that throughout the long agony of eight terrible hours the Allied line was literally pervaded by Wellington. Wherever danger threatened, there was the thorough bred chestnut horse and the erect figure in the saddle, wearing the low cocked hat, with the colours of Spain, Portugal and the Netherlands on the cockade, short blue cloak over a blue frock-coat and white leathers—the keen grey eyes always alert, the mouth inflexibly firm, and the expression unchangeably serene. Now he was heartening some hardly-pressed British battalion, now rallying some broken auxiliaries, now leading some young Hanoverians from the second line into the first; and in the lulls, when the musketry was silent and the French artillery was tearing up the front, he would send his staff to the reverse slope and, attended by one officer only, would stand in the full tempest of shot and shell gazing at the French troops on the other side of the valley. He was one who was never demonstrative in any circumstances, who said little and was sparing of gesture.

But his mere presence diffused an atmosphere of calm and confidence, and all who were aware of it thanked God and took courage. His eye too was everywhere. It caught sight of a French gun-carriage flying to splinters under the blow of an English shot; and away flew an *aide-de-camp* to place under arrest the commander of a battery who had dared to fire at guns when the order was to fire only at men. Without Wellington the Allied line could never have endured to the end, and he was in a modest way aware of it. "It has been a damned nice thing," he told Creevey next day, " the nearest run thing that ever you saw in your life. By God," he added, as if thinking aloud, "I don't think it would have done if I had not been there."

The Prince of Orange on the morrow of the fight wrote anxiously to the duke "to know how he could explain or pass over the conduct of the Netherlands' troops." The duke answered, "I shall praise generally and not in detail, so nobody will know anything about them." There was glory enough, he said later, for everyone, and he spoke truly. There was not a nation among the Allies which had not at one period or another rendered transcendent service to the cause of Europe in that short campaign; and not one that had fought more valiantly than their most noble and gallant enemy. Had Waterloo not been a final and decisive battle, it would have been coupled with Albuera in the popular memory as a great feat of endurance and tenacity. But, though

PART OF FRANCE.
SECTION 1.
to illustrate the
ADVANCE OF THE ALLIED ARMIES.

PART OF FRANCE,
SECTION II
to illustrate the
ADVANCE OF THE ALLIED ARMIES.

0 5 10   20   40   60 Eng.Miles

———————— Army of the Upper Rhine.
•••••••••• Army of Italy.

Longitude East of

6 · 8 · 48

GERMANY

Semirementa · Freiburg · Schaffhausen
Langres · Mulhausen · Chaловы · Büningen · Constance
Besoul · Belfort · Donnemarie
Montbéliard · Basle · Rheinfeld · Zürich
Gray · Ognon · Doubs · Baume
Doubs · Bésançon · Solothurn · Lucerne
Dôle · R. Rhine
Salins · Neuchatel · BERNE
Pontarlier · SWITZERLAND
Lons le · Freiburg · Thun · R. Rhine
Saunier · Lausanne
ouhans · St. Laurent · Brig · R. Rhône · Sion
Les Rousses · Meillerie · St. Maurice
St. Claude · Geneva
Oyonnax · Ge. · St. Gingo
Chanc · Geneva · Bonneville · 46
Cralliers · de l'Écluse
Seyssel · R. Rhône
Aosta · Dora Baltea · Ivrea · R. Sesia · R. Rhône
Conflans · ITALY
Chambery · Moutiers · Vercelli
es Echelles · Montmélian · R. Po
Barraux · Suse · Dora Riparia · TURIN
Grenoble · R. Po
Briançon · R. Tanaro

Greenwich · 6 · 8

its fame may be partly obscured by later and more gigantic contests, it can never be wholly obliterated. Napoleons do not so frequently appear that the downfall of them and of the power that they have wielded can readily lose significance.

By a happy coincidence it occurred simultaneously to the commanders-in-chief in the field and at the Horse Guards that so heroic a fight and so momentous an occasion should be commemorated, for the first time since Dunbar, by the issue of a medal to every man in the army who had been present; and this medal is still the possession most highly treasured alike in the highest and the humblest of English homes. The design is of little merit, yet it is unique, and worthily unique, among British military medals, for it bears on the reverse, besides the name and date of the battle, the name of him without whom there would have been no victory—the one word Wellington.

Appendix 1

THE ANGLO-ALLIED ARMY IN THE WATERLOO CAMPAIGN

Commander-in-Chief.—Field-Marshal the Duke of Wellington, K.G.

Quarter-master-General.—Colonel Oliver De Lancey.

(G.) signifies regiments that had served with Graham in the Netherlands; (P.) regiments that had served in the Peninsular War.

FIRST CORPS (The Prince of Orange)

First Division (Maj.-Gen. Cooke).

1st British Brigade Maj.-Gen. Maitland	2/1st Guards (G.) 3/1st Guards
2nd British Brigade Maj.-Gen. Sir John Byng	2nd Coldstream Guards (G.) 2/3rd Guards (G.)

Artillery—Sandham's British and Kuhlmann's K.G.L. field-batteries.

Total—4061 infantry, 12 guns.

Third Division (Lieut.-Gen. Sir Charles Alten).

5th British Brigade Maj.-Gen. Sir Colin Halkett	2/30th (G.), 33rd (G.) 2/69th (G.), 2/73rd (G.)
2nd K.G.L. Brigade Col. von Ompteda	1st and 2nd Light Battalions K.G.L. 5th and 8th Line Battalions K.G.L.
1st Hanoverian Brigade Maj.-Gen. Count Kielmansegge	6 Hanoverian battalions

Artillery—Lloyd's British and Cleeves's K.G.L. field-batteries.

Total—6970 infantry, 12 guns.

Second Netherlandish Division (Lieut.-Gen. Baron de Perponcher).

1st Brigade
  Maj.-Gen. de Bijlandt } 5 Netherlandish battalions
2nd Brigade
  Prince Bernard of Saxe-Wiemar } 5 Nassau battalions

Artillery—One field-battery, Bijleveld's horse-battery.

Total—7700 infantry, 12 guns.

Third Netherlandish Division (Lieut.-Gen. Baron de Chassé).

1st Brigade
  Maj.-Gen. Detmers } 6 Netherlandish battalions
2nd Brigade
  Maj.-Gen. d'Aubremé } 6 Netherlandish battalions

Artillery—A field-battery and a horse-battery, Netherlandish.

Total—6669 infantry, 16 guns.

TOTAL FIRST CORPS—25,400 infantry, 56 guns.

SECOND CORPS (Lieut.-Gen. Lord Hill)

Second Division (Lieut.-Gen. Sir H. Clinton).

3rd British Brigade
  Maj.-Gen. Adam } 1/52nd (P.), 1/71st (P.) 2/95th (P.), 3/95th (G.)
1st K.G.L. Brigade
  Col. Du Plat } 1st, 2nd, 3rd, 4th Line Battalions K.G.L.
3rd Hanoverian Brigade
  Col. Hew Halkett } 4 Landwehr battalions

Artillery—Bolton's British and Sympher's K.G.L. field-batteries.

Total—6833 infantry, 12 guns.

Fourth Division (Lieut.-Gen. Sir C. Colville).

4th British Brigade
  Col. Mitchell } 3/14th, 1/23rd (P.), 51st (P.)
6th British Brigade
  Maj.-Gen. Johnstone } 2/35th (G.), 1/54th (G.) 59th, 1/91st (G.)
6th Hanoverian Brigade
  Maj.-Gen. Sir James Lyon } 5 Hanoverian battalions

Artillery—Brome's British and Rettberg's Hanoverian field-batteries.

Total—7217 infantry, 12 guns.

Corps of Prince Frederick of the Netherlands.

1st Netherlandish Division ⎫ D'Hauw's Brigade, 6 battalions
Lieut.-Gen. Stedman ⎭ De Eerens's Brigade, 5 battalions

Total—6437 infantry, and one field-battery of 8 guns.

Anthing's Netherland ⎫ 5 battalions and 1 field-battery
Indian Brigade ⎭

Total—3499 infantry, 8 guns.

TOTAL SECOND CORPS—23,986 infantry, 40 guns.

CAVALRY

1st Brigade
  Maj.-Gen. Lord E.   1st and 2nd Life Guards, Blues
    Somerset
2nd Brigade
  Maj.-Gen. Sir W.   Royals, Greys, Inniskillings
    Ponsonby
3rd Brigade
  Maj.-Gen. Sir W.   1st and 2nd Light Dragoons K.G.L.
    Dörnberg   23rd Light Dragoons
4th Brigade
  Maj.-Gen. Sir J.   11th, 12th, 16th Light Dragoons
    Vandeleur
5th Brigade
  Maj.-Gen. Sir   7th and 15th Hussars
    Colquhoun Grant   2nd Hussars K.G.L.
6th Brigade
  Maj.-Gen. Sir Hussey   10th and 18th Hussars
    Vivian   1st Hussars K.G.L.
7th Brigade   13th Light Dragoons
  Col. Arentschild   3rd Hussars K.G.L.

Artillery — Bull's (howitzers), Gardiner's, Mercer's, Ramsay's, Webler-Smith's, and Whinyates's horse-batteries.

Total—8471 cavalry, 36 guns.

1st Hanoverian Cavalry ⎫ 3 regiments, 1682 men
Brigade ⎭

Brunswick Cavalry ⎫ 1 regiment and 1 squadron, 922
            ⎭ cavalry

Netherlandish Cavalry ⎫ 3 brigades (Trip, de Ghigny, Van
            ⎬ Merlen), 7 regiments, and 2 half-
            ⎭ batteries

Total—3405 cavalry and 8 guns.

TOTAL CAVALRY—14,482 and 44 guns.

Seventh Division.

7th British Brigade   } 2/25th (G.), 2/37th (G.), 2/78th (G.)
                       } 3 British garrison battalions.

Total—3233 men.

Hanoverian Reserve Corps   12 Landwehr battalions in 4 brigades

Total—9000 men.

TOTAL GARRISONS—12,233 men.

GRAND TOTAL (including 1240 Engineers and waggon-train)—
105,834 men and 204 guns.

RESERVE

Fifth Division (Lieut-Gen. Sir Thomas Picton).

8th British Brigade | 1/28th (P.), 1/32nd (P.)
  Maj.-Gen. Sir James | 1/79th (P.), 1/95th (P.)
  Kempt |
9th British Brigade | 3/1st (P.), 1/42nd (P.)
  Maj.-Gen. Sir Denis | 2/44th (P.), 1/92nd (P.)
  Pack |
5th Hanoverian Brigade | 4 Landwehr battalions
  Col. von Vincke |

Artillery—Rogers's British and Braun's Hanoverian field-batteries.

Total—7158 infantry, 12 guns.

Sixth Division.

10th British Brigade | 1/4th (P.)., 1/27th (P.)
  Maj.-Gen. Sir John | 1/40th (P.), 2/81st (P.)
  Lambert |
4th Hanoverian Brigade | 4 Landwehr battalions
  Col. Best |

Artillery—Unett's and Sinclair's field-batteries.

Total—5149 infantry, 12 guns.

British Reserve Artillery.

  2 horse-batteries (Ross and Bean).
  3 field-batteries (Morisson, Hutcheson, Ilbert).

Brunswick Corps (The Duke of Brunswick).

  Advanced guard, 4 companies infantry, detachment cavalry, 2
  brigades (each 3 battalions), and 2 batteries.

Total—5376 infantry and 16 guns.

Nassau Contingent (General von Kruse), 3 battalions.

Total—2841 infantry.

TOTAL RESERVE—20,524 infantry, 64 guns.

TOTAL STRENGTH BY NATIONALITIES

Nation.	Infantry.		Cavalry.		Guns.
British .	20,310 rank and file		5,911 rank and file		90
K.G.L.	3,285 ,,	,,	2,560 ,,	,,	18
Hanoverians .	13,793 ,,	,,	1,682 .,	,,	12
Brunswick .	5,376 ,,	,,	922 ,,	,,	16
Nassau .	7,308 all ranks		...		...
Netherlanders	18,838 ,,		3,405 all ranks		56
	68,910		14,480		192

(Taken from *The Campaign of 1815*, by Lieut.-Col. W. H. James.)

Appendix 2

STRENGTH OF THE BRITISH ARMY PRESENT AT WATERLOO

(Abridged from the Field-State printed by Siborne, which, however, seems from internal evidence to be imperfect.)

Division	Brigade	Regiments	Officers	Other ranks
		R.A.	175	4769
		K.G.L. Art.	25	546
		R.E.	37	...
		Sappers & Miners	10	735
		Waggon-Train	16	285
		Staff Corps	18	251
Cav.	1st	1st L.G.	16	229
		2nd L.G.	20	215
		Blues	19	232
		K.D.G.	29	568
	2nd	1st. D.	30	398
		2nd D.	28	414
		6th D.	26	419
	3rd	1st L.D.K.G.L.	34	500
		2nd L.D.K.G.L.	33	472
		3rd L.D.	28	313
	4th	11th L.D.	27	408
		12th L.D.	26	401
		16th L.D.	30	403
	5th	7th Hrs.	18	344
		15th Hrs.	28	419
		3rd Hrs. K.G.L.	36	547
	6th	10th Hrs.	26	426
		18th Hrs.	25	417
		1st Hrs. K.G.L.	36	550
		13th L.D.	28	420
		3rd Hrs. K.G.L.	37	647

Division	Brigade	Regiments	Officers	Other ranks
		INFANTRY.		
1st	1st Brit.	2/1st Gds.	29	752
		3/1st Gds.	29	818
	2nd Brit.	2/C. Gds.	36	1006
		2/3rd Gds.	34	1021
3rd	5th Brit.	2/30th	40	593
		1/33rd	31	535
		2/69th	30	511
		2/73rd	23	475
	2nd K.G.L.	5th Line K.G.L.	31	471
		8th Line K.G.L.	32	513
		1st Light K.G.L.	32	458
		2nd Light K.G.L.	31	406
2nd	3rd Brit.	1/52nd	59	1079
		1/71st	50	931
		Det. 3/95th	10	193
		2/95th	34	621
	1st K.G.L.	1st Line K.G.L.	29	426
		2nd Line K.G.L.	29	463
		3rd Line K.G.L.	30	553
		4th Line K.G.L.	30	448
5th	4th Brit.	3/14th	38	592
		1/23rd	44	647
		1/51st	45	474
	8th Brit.	1/28th	35	521
		1/32nd	26	477
		1/79th	26	414
		1/95th	17	401
	9th Brit.	3/1st	36	417
		1/42nd	17	312
		2/44th	20	450
		1/92nd	22	400
	10th Brit.	1/4th	27	643
		1/27th	21	729
		1/40th	43	819

Appendix 3

COMPOSITION OF THE PRUSSIAN ARMY UNDER FIELD-MARSHAL PRINCE VON BLÜCHER

Chief of Staff.—Lieut.-General Count von Gneisenau.
Quarter-master-General.—Major-General von Grolmann.

Ist Army Corps (Lieut.-Gen. von Ziethen)

1st Brigade	Steinmetz	9069 men	16 guns
2nd ,,	Pirch II.	8018 ,,	18 ,,
3rd ,,	Jagow	7146 ,,	8 ,,
4th ,,	Henckel	4900 ,,	8 ,,
Reserve Cavalry	Röder	2175 ,,	8 ,,
Reserve Artillery	Rentzell		30 ,,

Total Ist Corps—31,308 men, 88 guns.

IInd Army Corps (Gen. von Pirch I.)

5th Brigade	Tippelskirch	7153 men	8 guns
6th ,,	Krafft	6762 ,,	8 ,,
7th ,,	Brause	6503 ,,	8 ,,
8th ,,	Bose	6584 ,,	8 ,,
Reserve Cavalry	Wahlen	4471 ,,	8 ,,
Reserve Artillery			32 ,,

Total IInd Corps—31,473 men, 72 guns.

IIIrd Army Corps (Lieut.-Gen. von Thielmann)

9th Brigade	Borcke	7262 men	8 guns
10th ,,	Kemphen	4419 ,,	8 ,,
11th ,,	Lück	3980 ,,	8 ,,
12th ,,	Stulpnagel	6614 ,,	8 ,,
Reserve Cavalry	Hobe	1981 ,,	8 ,,
Reserve Artillery	Grevenitz		16 ,,

Total IIIrd Corps—24,256 men, 56 guns.

IVᵗʰ Corps (Gen. Count Bülow)

13th Brigade .	. Hake . .	. 6560 men	8 guns
14th ,,	. Ryssel . .	. 7138 ,,	8 ,,
15th ,,	. Losthin . .	. 7143 ,,	8 ,,
16th ,,	. Hiller . .	. 6423 ,,	8 ,,
Reserve Cavalry	. Prince William	. 3321 ,,	16 ,,
Reserve Artillery	. Bardeben . .	. .	. 32 ,,

Total IVth Corps—30,585 men, 80 guns.

SUMMARY

Ist Corps .	. 27,817 infantry	2,675 cavalry	88 guns
IInd Corps	. 25,836 ,,	4,471 ,,	72 ,,
IIIrd Corps	. 20,611 ,,	2,581 ,,	56 ,,
IVth Corps	. 25,381 ,,	3,921 ,,	80 ,,
Total .	. 99,645 ,,	13,648 ,,	296 ,,

(exclusive of gunners, engineers, and train.)

(Abstracted from Appendix to *The Campaign of 1815*, by Lieut-Col. W. H. James.)

Appendix 4

COMPOSITION OF THE FRENCH ARMY UNDER THE EMPEROR NAPOLEON

Chief of Staff.—Marshal Soult, Duke of Dalmatia.

IMPERIAL GUARD (DROUOT)

Infantry.   Men.

Friant—1st, 2nd, 3rd, 4th Grenadiers 4,140
Morand—1st, 2nd, 3rd, 4th Chasseurs 4,603
Duhesme—1st, 2nd Tirailleurs, 1st, 2nd Voltigeurs . . 4,283

Total Infantry . . . 13,026

Cavalry.

Lefebvre Desnoëttes—Lancers and Mounted Chasseurs ⎫
Guyot—Dragoons and Horse Grenadiers . . ⎬ 4100
D'Autancourt—Gendarmerie d'Élite . . . . ⎭

Artillery.

Desvaux—13 foot- and 3 horse-batteries.
Engineers and sailors of the Guard.

Total—20,755 men, 122 guns.

FIRST CORPS D'ARMÉE (D'ERLON)

First Division. Quiot.	? Brigade, 54th, 55th Line Bourgeois's Brigade, 28th, 105th Line	4000
Second Division. Douzelot.	Schmitz's Brigade, 13th Light, 17th Line Aulard's Brigade, 19th, 51st Line	5132
Third Division. Marcognet.	Noguez's Brigade, 21st, 46th Line Grenier's Brigade, 25th, 45th Line	3900

		Men.
Fourth Division. Durutte.	Pégot's Brigade, 8th, 29th Line Brue's Brigade, 58th, 95th Line	}3853
First Cavalry Division. Jacquinot.	Bruno's Brigade } 3rd Chass., 7th Hussars Gobrecht's Brigade } 3rd, 4th Lancers	}1706

Artillery—5 foot-batteries, 1 horse-battery.

Engineers—5 companies.

Total (with train)—20,731 men, 46 guns.

SECOND CORPS D'ARMÉE (REILLE)

		Men.
Fifth Division. Bachelu.	Husson's Brigade, 2nd Light, 61st Line Campy's Brigade, 72nd, 108th Line	}4103
Sixth Division. Jérôme Bonaparte.	Bauduin's Brigade, 1st, 3rd Light Soye's Brigade, 1st, 2nd Line	}7819
Seventh Division. Girard.	Devilliers's Brigade, 11th Light, 82nd Line Piat's Brigade, 12th Light, 4th Line	}3925
Ninth Division. Foy.	Gauthier's Brigade, 92nd, 93rd Line B. Jamin's Brigade, 4th Light, 100th Line	}4788
Second Cavalry Division. Piré.	Huberts's Brigade, 1st, 6th Chasseurs Vathiez's Brigade, 5th, 6th Lancers	}2064

Artillery—5 foot-batteries, 1 horse-battery.

Engineers—5 companies.

Total (with train)—25,179 men, 46 guns.

THIRD CORPS D'ARMÉE (VANDAMME)

		Men.
Eighth Division. Lefol.	Billard's Brigade, 15th Light, 23rd Line Corsin's Brigade, 37th, 64th Line	}4541
Tenth Division. Habert.	Gengoux's Brigade, 34th, 88th Line Dupeyroux's Brigade, 22nd, 70th Line 2nd Swiss Foreign Legion	}5024

200

	Men.
Eleventh Division. Berthezène.	Dufour's Brigade, 12th, 56th Line Lagarde's Brigade, 33rd, 86th Line	} 5565
Third Cavalry Division. Domont.	Dommanget's Brigade, 4th, 9th Chasseurs Vinot's Brigade, 12th Chasseurs	} 1017

Artillery—4 foot-batteries, 1 horse-battery.

Engineers—3 companies.

Total (with train)—18,105 men, 46 guns.

Fourth Corps d'Armée (Gérard)

Twelfth Division. Pécheux.	Romme's Brigade, 30th, 96th Line Schœffer's Brigade, 6th Light, 63rd Line	} 4719
Thirteenth Division. Vichéry.	Le Capitaine's Brigade, 59th, 76th Line Desprez's Brigade, 48th, 60th Line	} 4145
Fourteenth Division. Bourmont.	Hulot's Brigade, 9th Light, 11th Line Toussaint's Brigade, 44th, 50th Line	} 4237
Seventh Cavalry Division. Maurin.	Vallin's Brigade, 6th Hussars, 8th Chasseurs Berruyer's Brigade, 6th, 16th Dragoons	} 1500

Artillery—5 foot-batteries, 1 horse-battery.

Engineers—3 companies.

Total (with train)—16,219 men, 46 guns.

Sixth Corps d'Armée (Lobau)

Nineteenth Division. Simmer.	Bellair's Brigade, 5th, 11th Line M. Jamin's Brigade, 27th, 84th Line	} 3953
Twentieth Division. Jannin.	Bony's Brigade, 5th Light, 10th Line Tromelin's Brigade, 47th, 107th Line	} 2202

Twenty-first Division. Teste.

{ Lafitte's Brigade, 8th Light, 40th Line
  Penne's Brigade, 65th, 75th Line } 2418

Artillery—4 foot-batteries.

Engineers—3 companies.

Total (with train)—10,821 men, 32 guns.

RESERVE CAVALRY (MARSHAL GROUCHY)

FIRST CAVALRY CORPS (PAJOL)

Fourth Cavalry Division. P. Soult.

St. Laurent's Brigade } 1st, 4th, 5th Hussars
Ameil's Brigade

Fifth Cavalry Division. Subervic.

A. de Colbert's Brigade, 1st, 2nd Lancers
Merlin's Brigade, 11th Chasseurs

} 2536

Artillery—2 horse-batteries.

SECOND CAVALRY CORPS (EXELMANS)

Ninth Cavalry Division. Strolz.

Burthe's Brigade, 5th, 13th Dragoons
Vincent's Brigade, 15th, 20th Dragoons

Tenth Cavalry Division. Chastel.

Bonnemains's Brigade, 4th, 12th Dragoons
Berton's Brigade, 14th, 17th Dragoons

} 3116

Artillery—2 horse-batteries.

THIRD CAVALRY CORPS (KELLERMANN)

Eleventh Cavalry Division. l'Héritier.

Piquet's Brigade, 2nd, 7th Dragoons
Guiton's Brigade, 8th, 11th Cuirassiers

Twelfth Cavalry Division. Roussel d'Harbal.

Blancard's Brigade, 1st, 2nd Carbineers
Donop's Brigade, 2nd, 3rd Cuirassiers

} 3400

Artillery—2 horse-batteries.

FOURTH CAVALRY CORPS (MILHAUD)

Men.

Thirteenth
Cavalry
Division.
Wathier.
{ Dubois's Brigade, 1st, 4th Cuirassiers
Travers's Brigade, 7th, 12th Cuirassiers

Fourteenth
Cavalry
Division.
Delort.
{ Farine's Brigade, 5th, 10th Cuirassiers
Vial's Brigade, 6th, 9th Cuirassiers

} 2797

Artillery—2 horse-batteries.

TOTAL RESERVE CAVALRY—11,849 men (without train), 48 guns.

SUMMARY

	Infantry.	Cavalry.	Artillery.	Engineers, etc	Guns.
Imperial Guard .	. 13,026	4,100	2,786	109	122
1st Corps d'Armée	. 16,885	1,706	1,096	330	46
2nd ,, ,,	. 20,635	2,064	1,700	409	46
3rd ,, ,,	. 15,130	1,017	1,084	146	38
4th ,, ,,	. 13,401	1,500	1,417	201	38
6th ,, ,,	. 8,573	...	765	189	32
Reserve Cavalry .	. ...	11,849	1,222	...	48
Total .	. 87,650	22,236	10,070	1,384	370

Grand Total (including train)—124,139 men, 370 guns.

(Abridged from Appendix to *The Campaign of 1815*, by
Lieut.-Col. W. H. James.)

LEONAUR

ALSO FROM LEONAUR
AVAILABLE IN SOFTCOVER OR HARDCOVER WITH DUST JACKET

THE FALL OF THE MOGHUL EMPIRE OF HINDUSTAN *by H. G. Keene*—By the beginning of the nineteenth century, as British and Indian armies under Lake and Wellesley dominated the scene, a little over half a century of conflict brought the Moghul Empire to its knees.

LADY SALE'S AFGHANISTAN *by Florentia Sale*—An Indomitable Victorian Lady's Account of the Retreat from Kabul During the First Afghan War.

THE CAMPAIGN OF MAGENTA AND SOLFERINO 1859 *by Harold Carmichael Wylly*—The Decisive Conflict for the Unification of Italy.

FRENCH'S CAVALRY CAMPAIGN *by J. G. Maydon*—A Special Correspondent's View of British Army Mounted Troops During the Boer War.

CAVALRY AT WATERLOO *by Sir Evelyn Wood*—British Mounted Troops During the Campaign of 1815.

THE SUBALTERN *by George Robert Gleig*—The Experiences of an Officer of the 85th Light Infantry During the Peninsular War.

NAPOLEON AT BAY, 1814 *by F. Loraine Petre*—The Campaigns to the Fall of the First Empire.

NAPOLEON AND THE CAMPAIGN OF 1806 *by Colonel Vachée*—The Napoleonic Method of Organisation and Command to the Battles of Jena & Auerstädt.

THE COMPLETE ADVENTURES IN THE CONNAUGHT RANGERS *by William Grattan*—The 88th Regiment during the Napoleonic Wars by a Serving Officer.

BUGLER AND OFFICER OF THE RIFLES *by William Green & Harry Smith*—With the 95th (Rifles) during the Peninsular & Waterloo Campaigns of the Napoleonic Wars.

NAPOLEONIC WAR STORIES *by Sir Arthur Quiller-Couch*—Tales of soldiers, spies, battles & sieges from the Peninsular & Waterloo campaigns.

CAPTAIN OF THE 95TH (RIFLES) *by Jonathan Leach*—An officer of Wellington's sharpshooters during the Peninsular, South of France and Waterloo campaigns of the Napoleonic wars.

RIFLEMAN COSTELLO *by Edward Costello*—The adventures of a soldier of the 95th (Rifles) in the Peninsular & Waterloo Campaigns of the Napoleonic wars.

LEONAUR

ALSO FROM LEONAUR
AVAILABLE IN SOFTCOVER OR HARDCOVER WITH DUST JACKET

ZULU:1879 *by D.C.F. Moodie & the Leonaur Editors*—The Anglo-Zulu War of 1879 from contemporary sources: First Hand Accounts, Interviews, Dispatches, Official Documents & Newspaper Reports.

THE RED DRAGOON *by W.J. Adams*—With the 7th Dragoon Guards in the Cape of Good Hope against the Boers & the Kaffir tribes during the 'war of the axe' 1843-48'.

THE RECOLLECTIONS OF SKINNER OF SKINNER'S HORSE *by James Skinner*—James Skinner and his 'Yellow Boys' Irregular cavalry in the wars of India between the British, Mahratta, Rajput, Mogul, Sikh & Pindarree Forces.

A CAVALRY OFFICER DURING THE SEPOY REVOLT *by A. R. D. Mackenzie*—Experiences with the 3rd Bengal Light Cavalry, the Guides and Sikh Irregular Cavalry from the outbreak to Delhi and Lucknow.

A NORFOLK SOLDIER IN THE FIRST SIKH WAR *by J W Baldwin*—Experiences of a private of H.M. 9th Regiment of Foot in the battles for the Punjab, India 1845-6.

TOMMY ATKINS' WAR STORIES: 14 FIRST HAND ACCOUNTS—Fourteen first hand accounts from the ranks of the British Army during Queen Victoria's Empire.

THE WATERLOO LETTERS *by H. T. Siborne*—Accounts of the Battle by British Officers for its Foremost Historian.

NEY: GENERAL OF CAVALRY VOLUME 1—1769-1799 *by Antoine Bulos*—The Early Career of a Marshal of the First Empire.

NEY: MARSHAL OF FRANCE VOLUME 2—1799-1805 *by Antoine Bulos*—The Early Career of a Marshal of the First Empire.

AIDE-DE-CAMP TO NAPOLEON *by Philippe-Paul de Ségur*—For anyone interested in the Napoleonic Wars this book, written by one who was intimate with the strategies and machinations of the Emperor, will be essential reading.

TWILIGHT OF EMPIRE *by Sir Thomas Ussher & Sir George Cockburn*—Two accounts of Napoleon's Journeys in Exile to Elba and St. Helena: Narrative of Events by Sir Thomas Ussher & Napoleon's Last Voyage: Extract of a diary by Sir George Cockburn.

PRIVATE WHEELER *by William Wheeler*—The letters of a soldier of the 51st Light Infantry during the Peninsular War & at Waterloo.

ALSO FROM LEONAUR
AVAILABLE IN SOFTCOVER OR HARDCOVER WITH DUST JACKET

OFFICERS & GENTLEMEN *by Peter Hawker & William Graham*—Two Accounts of British Officers During the Peninsula War: Officer of Light Dragoons by Peter Hawker & Campaign in Portugal and Spain by William Graham .

THE WALCHEREN EXPEDITION *by Anonymous*—The Experiences of a British Officer of the 81st Regt. During the Campaign in the Low Countries of 1809.

LADIES OF WATERLOO *by Charlotte A. Eaton, Magdalene de Lancey & Juana Smith*—The Experiences of Three Women During the Campaign of 1815: Waterloo Days by Charlotte A. Eaton, A Week at Waterloo by Magdalene de Lancey & Juana's Story by Juana Smith.

JOURNAL OF AN OFFICER IN THE KING'S GERMAN LEGION *by John Frederick Hering*—Recollections of Campaigning During the Napoleonic Wars.

JOURNAL OF AN ARMY SURGEON IN THE PENINSULAR WAR *by Charles Boutflower*—The Recollections of a British Army Medical Man on Campaign During the Napoleonic Wars.

ON CAMPAIGN WITH MOORE AND WELLINGTON *by Anthony Hamilton*—The Experiences of a Soldier of the 43rd Regiment During the Peninsular War.

THE ROAD TO AUSTERLITZ *by R. G. Burton*—Napoleon's Campaign of 1805.

SOLDIERS OF NAPOLEON *by A. J. Doisy De Villargennes & Arthur Chuquet*—The Experiences of the Men of the French First Empire: Under the Eagles by A. J. Doisy De Villargennes & Voices of 1812 by Arthur Chuquet .

INVASION OF FRANCE, 1814 *by F. W. O. Maycock*—The Final Battles of the Napoleonic First Empire.

LEIPZIG—A CONFLICT OF TITANS *by Frederic Shoberl*—A Personal Experience of the 'Battle of the Nations' During the Napoleonic Wars, October 14th-19th, 1813.

SLASHERS *by Charles Cadell*—The Campaigns of the 28th Regiment of Foot During the Napoleonic Wars by a Serving Officer.

BATTLE IMPERIAL *by Charles William Vane*—The Campaigns in Germany & France for the Defeat of Napoleon 1813-1814.

SWIFT & BOLD *by Gibbes Rigaud*—The 60th Rifles During the Peninsula War.

www.ingramcontent.com/pod-product-compliance
Lightning Source LLC
Chambersburg PA
CBHW032057080426
42733CB00006B/317